Better Homes and Gardens®

GAS GRILL
Cookbook

Better Homes and Gardens® Books
Des Moines, Iowa

All of us at Better Homes and Gardens® Books are dedicated to providing you with the information and ideas you need to create delicious foods. We welcome your comments and suggestions. Write to us at Better Homes and Gardens Books, Cookbook Editorial Department, 1716 Locust St., Des Moines, IA 50309-3023.

If you would like to purchase any of our books, check wherever quality books are sold. Visit our website at bhg.books.com or bhg.com.

Our seal assures you that every recipe in the *Gas Grill Cookbook* has been tested in the Better Homes and Gardens® Test Kitchen. This means that each recipe is practical and reliable, and meets our high standards of taste appeal. We guarantee your satisfaction with this book for as long as you own it.

Pictured on front cover: Apricot Teriyaki Glaze on chicken, page 82

Cover Photo: Pete Krumhardt, Photographer; Dianna Nolin, Food Stylist

Better Homes and Gardens® Books
An imprint of Meredith® Books

Gas Grill Cookbook
Editor: Jennifer Dorland Darling
Project Manager and Writer: Lisa Kingsley
Recipe Developers: Brett Champion, Jim Fobel, Rosemary Mark
Associate Art Director: Lynda Haupert
Copy Chief: Catherine Hamrick
Copy and Production Editor: Terri Fredrickson
Managers, Book Production: Pam Kvitne, Marjorie J. Schenkelberg
Contributing Copy Editor: Shirley Williams
Contributing Proofreaders: Marcy Hall, Susan J. Kling, Sherri Schultz
Electronic Production Coordinator: Paula Forest
Editorial and Design Assistants: Judy Bailey, Mary Lee Gavin, Karen Schirm
Test Kitchen Director: Lynn Blanchard
Test Kitchen Product Supervisor: Marilyn Cornelius
Test Kitchen Home Economists: Patricia Beebout, Judy Comstock, Maryellyn Krantz, Tami Leonard, Jan Miller, R.D., Jill Moberly, Jennifer Peterson, Kay Springer, Colleen Weeden, Lori Wilson, Charles Worthington

Meredith® Books
Editor in Chief: James D. Blume
Design Director: Matt Strelecki
Managing Editor: Gregory H. Kayko

Director, Retail Sales and Marketing: Terry Unsworth
Director, Sales, Special Markets: Rita McMullen
Director, Sales, Premiums: Michael A. Peterson
Director, Sales, Retail: Tom Wierzbicki
Director, Book Marketing: Brad Elmitt
Director, Operations: George A. Susral
Director, Production: Douglas M. Johnston

Vice President, General Manager: Jamie L. Martin

Better Homes and Gardens® Magazine
Editor in Chief: Jean LemMon
Executive Food Editor: Nancy Byal

Meredith Publishing Group
President, Publishing Group: Christopher M. Little
Vice President, Finance & Administration: Max Runciman

Meredith Corporation
Chairman and Chief Executive Officer: William T. Kerr

Chairman of the Executive Committee: E. T. Meredith III

Contents

Welcome to Our Kitchen 4

Gas-Grill Savvy 5

Beef, Pork, & Lamb 7

Poultry 27

Fish & Seafood 41

Burgers & Sandwiches 53

Starters, Sides, & Sweets 65

Sauces & More 79

Smoking 85

Index 93

Metric Information 96

Grilling Charts
(see inside front & back covers)

Welcome to Our Kitchen

When you cook with a Better Homes and Gardens® cookbook, you can be confident that every recipe will taste great every time. That's because we perfect every recipe in our Test Kitchen before we present it to you.

Since the 1950s, when *Better Homes and Gardens* magazine first introduced the idea of the backyard "barbecue" to its readers, millions of Americans have been firing up the grill and cooking in the great outdoors. Throughout the years, they've relied on the Better Homes and Gardens® Test Kitchen for great grilling recipes, tips, and up-to-date product and safety information.

Grilling is more popular than ever—and of the millions of grills dotting backyards across the country, the great majority are gas. Their convenience, ease, and less-mess factor mean they're used twice as often as charcoal grills. If you own a gas grill, the *Better Homes and Gardens Gas Grill Cookbook* is a must-have.

Every recipe was written specifically for gas grills and tested on units including Kenmore, Weber, Ducane, Sunbeam, and Coleman. For spontaneous or last-minute grilling, charts on the front and back inside covers provide timings for meat, poultry, vegetables, and fish and seafood. Just pair one with a sauce, rub, or salsa from the Sauces & More chapter. Depending on your mood, maybe it's Mango-Mint Salsa, Indian Curry Rub, or Apricot Teriyaki Glaze.

Tips throughout the book provide information on ingredients, grilling methods, and such subjects as smoke-cooking on your gas grill. If you're looking for low-fat recipes, look for ♥. This symbol identifies main-dish recipes with 10 grams or less of total fat.

It may be our job to make recipes, but remember—we're cooks at home, too. What you want in a recipe, we want: great taste and terrific ease. Every day, we work to that end. We think the *Gas Grill Cookbook* is full of great recipes. We think you will, too.

Lynn Blanchard

Lynn Blanchard
Better Homes and Gardens®
Test Kitchen Director

Gas-Grill Savvy

Professional cooks get a lot of cooking questions. When the Better Homes and Gardens® Test Kitchen Home Economists get a grilling question from readers, they research and recipe-test to find the answer—and they have lots of them. Here are their answers to some of the most-asked questions.

Q.

Is it necessary to preheat my gas grill?

A.

Generally, you should let your gas grill preheat for 10 to 15 minutes before you put the food on it. Follow the recommendations for preheating given in the owner's manual for your particular grill.

Q.

If my grill burner doesn't start right away, what should I do?

A.

If the burners don't ignite on the first try, leave the grill hood open and turn off the gas. Wait about 5 minutes before trying again. Also, be sure there is fuel in the tank.

Q.

How can I avoid excess charring on the surface of my food?

A.

You could be cooking at too high a temperature. Or perhaps you are cooking directly over the heat source when you should be using the indirect method of grilling. The direct method of grilling means foods are placed directly over the heat source. It's best suited to smaller, thinner cuts of meat, poultry, or fish—foods that cook in 20 minutes or less. The indirect method of grilling means foods are placed adjacent to the heat source. Indirect grilling is best suited to larger cuts of meat, such as ribs, roasts, whole birds, and longer-cooking vegetables such as corn on the cob. You might need to hold off on brushing the barbecue sauce on your foods, too. Sauces that contain sugar tend to burn quickly, so brush them on only during the last 5 to 10 minutes of grilling.

Q.

When should I cook with the grill cover on? When should it be off?

A.

The manufacturers of nearly all gas grills recommend that the lid should always be closed when you cook on a gas grill.

Q.

If I don't have a thermometer on my grill, how do I know medium heat from high heat?

A.

Although most newer gas grills come with a high-medium-low heat indicator, if you have an older model, you might not have that convenience. Here's how to tell how hot your grill is: Hold your hand where the food will cook for as long as it's comfortable. The number of seconds you can hold it there gives you an approximate temperature.

Number of seconds	Temperature
2	High (400° to 450°)
3	Medium-high (375° to 400°)
4	Medium (350° to 375°)
5	Medium-low (300° to 350°)
6	Low (300° and lower)

Q.

When turning off the grill, do I turn off the gas source or the burner first?

A.

Turn off the gas source first. The burner will go out, and remember to turn it off, too.

Q.

What kind of maintenance do I need to do on my gas grill?

A.

To make seasonal cleaning easier, every time you grill, burn off any residue left on the grill rack by turning all the burners to high for 10 to 20 minutes, then brush the grill rack with a wire grill brush. Do the following at least once a season—and be sure the grill is turned off and cold: Change the catch-pan liner and clean the warming racks and control panel with a soapy fine steel-wool pad (use a light touch to avoid scratching) to remove smoke stains and burned-on food and grease. Rinse everything thoroughly with clear water. Then remove the bottom tray from under the grill. Holding it over a trash can, carefully scrape the inside with a putty knife. Push any residue out through the bottom hole. Clean tough stuff left in the tray with a soapy fine steel-wool pad and a very light touch. Do not line the bottom tray with foil. Grease accumulates in the creases and can start a fire.

Beef, Pork, & Lamb

Thai Pork Satay

In This Chapter:

Basil-Stuffed Beef 16
Beef and Blue Cheese
    Salad 13
Filet Mignon with
    Peppercorn Sauce 14
Fragrant Minted Lamb
    Chops 24
Garlic-Barbecued
    Steaks 12
Grilled Greek Leg of
    Lamb 23

Grilled Steak with Martini
    Twist 10
Horseradish-Rubbed Beef
    Tenderloin 15
Jerk Pork 20
Mediterranean Veal
    Brochettes 26
Mexican Fiesta Flank
    Steak 11
Mongolian-Style Lamb
    Chops 25

Peppery Pork Chops 17
Rib Eyes with Grilled
    Garlic 9
South Carolina Barbecued
    Chops 19
Sweet and Spicy BBQ
    Ribs 22
Teriyaki T-Bone Steaks 8
Thai Pork Satay 21

Teriyaki T-Bone Steaks

The tangy-sweet taste of teriyaki flavors these he-man T-bones. Serve them with steamed rice tossed with toasted macadamia nuts and thinly sliced green onions.

Prep: 15 minutes **Marinate:** 4 hours **Grill:** 8 minutes **Serves:** 4 or 2

2   beef T-bone steaks, cut
    1 inch thick (1¾ to
    2 pounds total)

Marinade

⅓   cup teriyaki sauce

2   tablespoons sliced green
    onion

1   tablespoon honey

1   tablespoon lemon juice or
    rice vinegar

1   tablespoon finely chopped
    fresh ginger

1   teaspoon toasted sesame
    oil

1   clove garlic, minced

¼   teaspoon coarsely ground
    black pepper

1   small fresh pineapple, cut
    into wedges and cored

2 or 4 1-inch-thick slices
    tomato or sweet pepper

1   tablespoon cooking oil

1 Trim fat from steaks. Place steaks in a plastic bag set in a shallow dish. For marinade, in a small bowl combine teriyaki sauce, green onion, honey, lemon juice, fresh ginger, sesame oil, garlic, and black pepper. Pour over steaks; seal bag. Marinate in the refrigerator for 4 to 6 hours, turning bag occasionally. Drain steaks, reserving marinade.

2 Preheat gas grill. Reduce heat to medium. Place steaks on the grill rack directly over heat. Cover and grill until steaks are desired doneness, turning and brushing once with marinade halfway through grilling. (Allow 8 to 12 minutes for medium rare or 12 to 15 minutes for medium.)

3 While the steaks are grilling, brush pineapple wedges and tomato slices with cooking oil; add pineapple and tomato to grill. Cover and grill for 6 to 8 minutes or until slightly charred, turning once halfway through grilling. Serve the steaks whole or cut each steak in half. Serve with pineapple and tomato.

Nutrition Facts per serving (for 4 servings): 400 cal., 15 g total fat (5 g sat. fat), 74 mg chol., 1,001 mg sodium, 40 g carbo., 2 g fiber, 72 g pro.
Daily Values: 48% vit. C, 5% calcium, 21% iron

Rib Eyes with Grilled Garlic

Garlic—called "the stinking rose" by none other than Shakespeare—sweetens upon cooking. Be sure to grill up an extra garlic bulb to spread on hearty slices of toasted French or sourdough bread.

Prep: 10 minutes **Grill:** 14 minutes **Serves:** 4

1 whole head of garlic
2 tablespoons olive oil or cooking oil
1 tablespoon snipped fresh basil or ½ teaspoon dried basil, crushed
1 tablespoon snipped fresh rosemary or ½ teaspoon dried rosemary, crushed
2 12-ounce boneless beef rib eye steaks, cut 1 inch thick

1 Fold a 24×18-inch piece of heavy foil in half crosswise. Trim to make a 12-inch square. Remove the papery outer layers from garlic head. Cut off and discard about ½ inch from top of garlic head to expose the garlic cloves. Place garlic head in center of foil. Bring the foil up around the garlic on all sides, forming a cup. Drizzle garlic with oil; sprinkle with basil and rosemary. Twist the ends of the foil to completely enclose the garlic in the foil. Trim fat from steaks.

2 Preheat grill. Reduce heat to medium. Place steaks and packet of garlic on the grill rack directly over heat. Cover and grill until steaks are desired doneness, turning once halfway through grilling. (Allow 14 to 18 minutes for medium rare or 18 to 22 minutes for medium.)

3 Place steaks on a serving platter. Open packet of garlic. Drizzle oil from packet over steaks. Squeeze the softened cloves of garlic from head; spread over steaks. Season to taste with salt and pepper. Cut each steak in half.

Nutrition Facts per serving: 325 cal., 17 g total fat (5 g sat. fat), 81 mg chol., 91 mg sodium, 3 g carbo., 0 g fiber, 38 g pro.
Daily Values: 1% vit. A, 4% vit. C, 3% calcium, 17% iron

Grilled Steak with Martini Twist ♥

The essence of summertime sophistication, this soaked steak picks up the pleasantly piney taste of the gin in the marinade. Gin is made with juniper berries, which gives it a woodsy flavor.

Prep: 10 minutes **Marinate:** 30 minutes **Grill:** 14 minutes **Serves:** 4

 4 boneless beef top loin
     steaks, cut 1 inch thick
     (1¾ to 2 pounds total)
Marinade
 ¼ cup finely chopped green
     onions
 ¼ cup gin
 1 tablespoon olive oil
 1 teaspoon finely shredded
     lemon peel

 1 teaspoon tricolored
     peppercorns, crushed
 2 tablespoons sliced
     pimiento-stuffed green
     olives
     Lemon peel strips

1 Trim fat from steaks. Place steaks in a plastic bag set in a shallow dish. For marinade, in a small bowl stir together the green onions, gin, olive oil, and lemon peel. Pour over steaks; seal bag. Marinate in the refrigerator for 30 minutes, turning bag once. Drain steaks, discarding marinade. Press the crushed peppercorns onto both sides of the steaks.

2 Preheat gas grill. Reduce heat to medium. Place steaks on the grill rack directly over heat. Cover and grill until steaks are desired doneness, turning once halfway through grilling. (Allow 14 to 18 minutes for medium rare or 18 to 22 minutes for medium.) Season to taste with salt. Garnish the steaks with sliced olives and lemon peel strips.

Nutrition Facts per serving: 264 cal., 8 g total fat (2 g sat. fat), 93 mg chol., 201 mg sodium, .5 g carbo., .2 g fiber, 43 g pro.
Daily Values: 3% vit. C, 4% calcium, 25% iron

Mexican Fiesta Flank Steak

Sip a margarita while you wait for this south-of-the-border-style steak to come off the grill. Warm the tortillas in a foil packet the last few minutes of grilling.

Prep: 15 minutes **Marinate:** 12 hours **Grill:** 12 minutes **Serves:** 6

1 1½- to 2-pound beef flank steak or skirt steak

Marinade

½ cup finely chopped onion
½ cup snipped fresh cilantro
¼ cup lime or lemon juice
3 tablespoons olive oil
½ teaspoon salt
½ teaspoon ground cumin
½ teaspoon dried oregano, crushed
¼ to ½ teaspoon ground red pepper or 1 fresh or pickled jalapeño pepper, chopped

3 medium red, yellow, and/or green sweet peppers, quartered
6 flour tortillas
1 tomato, cut into thin wedges

1 Trim fat from steak. Score steak by making shallow diagonal cuts at 1-inch intervals in a diamond pattern. Repeat on other side. Place steak in a plastic bag set in a shallow dish.

2 For marinade, in a small bowl combine onion, cilantro, lime juice, 2 tablespoons of the olive oil, the salt, cumin, oregano, and ground red pepper. Pour over steak; seal bag. Marinate in the refrigerator for 12 to 24 hours, turning bag occasionally. Drain steak, discarding marinade.

3 Preheat gas grill. Reduce heat to medium. Place steak on the grill rack directly over heat. Cover and grill until steak is desired doneness, turning once halfway through grilling. (Allow 12 to 14 minutes for medium.)

4 While steak is grilling, brush sweet peppers with the remaining 1 tablespoon olive oil; add sweet peppers to grill. Cover and grill for 8 to 10 minutes or until tender and slightly charred, turning once halfway through grilling. Thinly slice steak across the grain. Slice sweet peppers into strips. Serve the steak and peppers with tortillas and tomato wedges.

Nutrition Facts per serving: 334 cal., 15 g total fat (4 g sat. fat), 45 mg chol., 314 mg sodium, 22 g carbo., 2 g fiber, 28 g pro.
Daily Values: 34% vit. A, 164% vit. C, 5% calcium, 18% iron

Garlic-Barbecued Steaks

Who has the best barbecue? You do, whether you're in Kansas City, Memphis, Houston—or Kalamazoo. All it takes are these garlic-studded steaks smothered in a sweet, easy sauce.

Prep: 20 minutes **Grill:** 14 minutes **Serves:** 4

2 boneless beef top loin or rib eye steaks, cut 1 inch thick (about 1½ pounds total)
2 large cloves garlic, thinly sliced
1 tablespoon olive oil
Salt and pepper

Sauce
¾ to 1 cup bottled barbecue sauce
1 tablespoon prepared mustard
1 tablespoon cider vinegar
1 tablespoon honey or brown sugar
1 teaspoon dried thyme, crushed

1 Trim fat from steaks. With the point of a paring knife, make small slits in steaks. Insert garlic into slits. Rub steaks with oil and sprinkle with salt and pepper. For sauce, in a small bowl stir together barbecue sauce, mustard, vinegar, honey, and thyme.

2 Preheat gas grill. Reduce heat to medium. Place steaks on the grill rack directly over heat. Cover and grill until steaks are desired doneness, turning and brushing once with sauce halfway through grilling. (Allow 14 to 18 minutes for medium rare or 18 to 22 minutes for medium.)

3 In a small saucepan bring the remaining sauce to boiling. Boil gently, uncovered, for 1 minute. Halve steaks to serve. Pass the sauce with steaks.

Nutrition Facts per serving: 301 cal., 12 g total fat (3 g sat. fat), 98 mg chol., 648 mg sodium, 11 g carbo., 1 g fiber, 34 g pro.
Daily Values: 10% vit. A, 6% vit. C, 3% calcium, 25% iron

safe grilling 101

There aren't many rules for using a gas grill, however following these few commonsense guidelines will help prevent accidents of any kind:

● Never grill indoors—not even in the garage—and never set up a grill on a wooden deck.

● Set up your grill on level ground far from the house, sidewalks, and places your children or pets might play. Keep it far away from any combustible materials.

● Lift the lid of the grill before turning on the gas to dilute the concentration of gas fumes, which can explode when lit. Turn off the gas before you do any kind of maintenance.

● Disconnect the gas tanks if you don't use your grill in winter, and never store gas tanks indoors.

Beef and Blue Cheese Salad

Like bread and wine, beef and blue cheese are born to be together. Substitute any blue-veined cheese—such as Roquefort or Maytag Blue—for the Gorgonzola.

Prep: 15 minutes **Grill:** 20 minutes **Serves:** 4

Vinaigrette
3 tablespoons balsamic vinegar
2 tablespoons olive oil
1 clove garlic, minced
½ teaspoon salt
½ teaspoon pepper

1 boneless beef sirloin steak, cut 1 inch thick (about 12 ounces)
1 tablespoon snipped fresh thyme
2 teaspoons snipped fresh rosemary
4 ¼-inch-thick slices red onion
6 cups lightly packed mesclun or torn mixed salad greens
8 yellow and/or red pear-shaped tomatoes, halved
2 tablespoons crumbled Gorgonzola or other blue cheese

1 For vinaigrette, in a screw-top jar combine vinegar, oil, garlic, salt, and pepper; cover and shake well. Trim fat from steak. Remove 1 tablespoon vinaigrette from jar and brush evenly onto both sides of the steak. Press thyme and rosemary onto both sides of the steak. Brush both sides of onion slices with some of the remaining vinaigrette, reserving the rest; set aside.

2 Preheat gas grill. Reduce heat to medium. Place steak on the grill rack directly over heat. Cover and grill until steak is desired doneness, turning once halfway through grilling. (Allow 20 to 24 minutes for medium rare or 24 to 28 minutes for medium.) While the steak is grilling, add onion slices to grill. Cover and grill for 6 to 8 minutes or until tender, turning once halfway through grilling.

3 Divide the mesclun among 4 dinner plates. To serve, thinly slice the steak across the grain. Separate onion slices into rings. Arrange warm steak slices and onion rings on top of mesclun. Drizzle with the reserved vinaigrette. Top with tomatoes and cheese.

Nutrition Facts per serving: 266 cal., 16 g total fat (5 g sat. fat), 59 mg chol., 373 mg sodium, 9 g carbo., 2 g fiber, 22 g pro.
Daily Values: 7% vit. A, 28% vit. C, 4% calcium, 22% iron

Filet Mignon with Peppercorn Sauce

Served with garlic mashed potatoes and the tiny, tender green beans called haricots verts, this bistro-style dish will have you speaking French with every forkful. Magnifique!

Prep: 10 minutes **Grill:** 14 minutes **Serves:** 2 or 3

2 or 3 six-ounce beef loin tenderloin steaks, cut 1 inch thick

1 teaspoon cracked black pepper

1 recipe Peppercorn-Mustard Sauce

1 Trim fat from steaks. Sprinkle cracked black pepper over both sides of steaks; press pepper onto steaks.

2 Preheat gas grill. Reduce heat to medium. Place steaks on the grill rack directly over heat. Cover and grill until steaks are desired doneness, turning once halfway through grilling. (Allow 14 to 18 minutes for medium rare or 18 to 22 minutes for medium.) Serve the steaks with Peppercorn-Mustard Sauce.

Peppercorn-Mustard Sauce: Mash 1 to 2 teaspoons drained pickled whole green peppercorns; set aside. In a small saucepan stir together ½ cup half-and-half or light cream, 1 tablespoon Dijon-style mustard, dash salt, and dash ground black pepper. Cook and stir over medium heat until slightly thickened and bubbly. Stir in the mashed peppercorns. Heat through.

Nutrition Facts per serving: 343 cal., 19 g total fat (8 g sat. fat), 107 mg chol., 261 mg sodium, 4 g carbo., 0 g fiber, 38 g pro.
Daily Values: 5% vit. A, 1% vit. C, 9% calcium, 28% iron

pick your pepper

Pepper is my favorite spice. It adds so much flavor to so many different foods.

Black pepper—the most common kind of pepper—is the berry of the pepper plant that's picked when not yet ripe, then dried. It has a hot-sweet flavor. White peppercorns are milder than the black ones. White peppercorns are the ripened berries of the pepper plant that are skinned and dried. Green peppercorns are underripe berries that are either dried or preserved in brine. The pickled peppercorns are soft and are milder than either black or white pepper.

Patty Bubout
Test Kitchen Home Economist

Horseradish-Rubbed Beef Tenderloin

This stunning dish featuring the classic complement of beef and horseradish suits any special occasion. Crisp popovers—fresh from the oven—are a must.

Prep: 10 minutes **Grill:** 45 minutes **Stand:** 15 minutes **Serves:** 10

1 2½- to 3-pound beef tenderloin
¼ cup prepared horseradish
½ teaspoon finely shredded lemon peel
2 teaspoons lemon juice
½ teaspoon coarsely cracked black pepper
3 tablespoons margarine or butter, melted

Sauce
⅓ cup dairy sour cream
1 tablespoon snipped fresh chives
¼ cup whipping cream, whipped

1 Trim fat from meat. In a small bowl combine horseradish, lemon peel, lemon juice, and pepper; reserve 2 tablespoons of the horseradish mixture. Stir melted margarine into remaining horseradish mixture. Brush margarine mixture onto meat. Insert a meat thermometer into center of meat.

2 Preheat gas grill. Adjust for indirect cooking over medium heat (see page 5). Place meat on a rack in a roasting pan; set the pan on the grill rack over unlit burner. Cover and grill for 45 to 60 minutes or until the meat thermometer registers 140° (medium rare). Remove meat from grill. Cover with foil; let stand for 15 minutes before slicing. (The meat's temperature will rise 5° during standing.)

3 Meanwhile, for sauce, in a small bowl stir together reserved horseradish mixture, the sour cream, and chives. Fold in whipped cream. To serve, thinly slice the meat across the grain. Pass the sauce with meat.

Nutrition Facts per serving: 248 cal., 16 g total fat (6 g sat. fat), 70 mg chol., 115 mg sodium, 1 g carbo., 0 g fiber, 24 g pro.
Daily Values: 8% vit. A, 2% vit. C, 3% calcium, 18% iron

Basil-Stuffed Beef

Slow cooking over indirect heat makes this top sirloin roast as tender as filet mignon. Slicing it reveals a surprise inside—an ambrosial stuffing of fresh basil and lots of garlic.

Prep: 20 minutes **Grill:** 1 hour **Stand:** 10 minutes **Serves:** 10 to 12

1 3- to 3½-pound boneless
beef top sirloin roast,
cut 1¾ inches thick
¼ teaspoon salt
¼ teaspoon pepper
Filling
2 cups loosely packed fresh
basil leaves, snipped
8 to 10 cloves garlic, minced

2 teaspoons olive oil

1 Trim fat from meat. Make five or six 5-inch-long slits along the top of the meat, cutting almost through it. Sprinkle with salt and pepper.

2 For filling, in a small bowl combine basil and garlic. Stuff the filling into the slits in the meat. Tie the meat with 100-percent-cotton string to hold the slits closed. Drizzle with olive oil. Insert a meat thermometer into center of meat.

3 Preheat gas grill. Adjust for indirect cooking over medium-low heat (see page 5). Place meat on a rack in a roasting pan; set the pan on the grill rack over unlit burner. Cover and grill for 1 to 1½ hours or until the meat thermometer registers 155° (medium). Remove meat from grill.

4 Cover with foil; let stand for 10 minutes before carving. (The meat's temperature will rise 5° during standing.)

Nutrition Facts per serving: 255 cal., 13 g total fat (5 g sat. fat), 91 mg chol., 121 mg sodium, 1 g carbo., 0 g fiber, 31 g pro.
Daily Values: 1% vit. C, 2% calcium, 23% iron

Peppery Pork Chops

Marinating these peppery chops the night before you plan to serve them makes quick work of a great dinner. Get some fried rice to go at your favorite Chinese spot, and dinner is done.

Prep: 15 minutes **Marinate:** 6 hours **Grill:** 20 minutes **Serves:** 4

4 center-cut pork loin chops, cut 1 inch thick

Marinade

¼ cup dry sherry

2 tablespoons soy sauce

2 tablespoons cooking oil

2 tablespoons grated fresh ginger

1 tablespoon sugar

1 tablespoon rice vinegar or lemon juice

1 large clove garlic, minced

¾ teaspoon coarsely ground black pepper

8 green onions (optional)

2 teaspoons cooking oil (optional)

Steamed or fried rice (optional)

1 Trim fat from pork chops. Place chops in a plastic bag set in a shallow dish. For marinade, in a small bowl combine sherry, soy sauce, the 2 tablespoons cooking oil, the ginger, sugar, rice vinegar, garlic, and pepper. Pour over chops; seal bag. Marinate in the refrigerator for 6 to 24 hours, turning bag occasionally. Drain pork chops, discarding marinade.

2 Preheat gas grill. Adjust for indirect cooking over medium heat (see page 5). Place chops on the grill rack over unlit burner. Cover and grill about 20 minutes or until an instant-read thermometer inserted in center registers 160°, turning once halfway through grilling.

3 While the chops are grilling, if using green onions, brush onions with the 2 teaspoons oil; add green onions to grill. Cover and grill about 2 minutes or until tender. If desired, serve the pork chops with the green onions and rice.

Nutrition Facts per serving: 255 cal., 11 g total fat (4 g sat. fat), 93 mg chol., 183 mg sodium, 1 g carbo., 0 g fiber, 35 g pro.
Daily Values: 1% vit. C, 4% calcium, 6% iron

South Carolina Barbecued Chops

Even from region to region within a state, the way meat is barbecued is different—and so are the sauces. True to form, this South Carolina-style sauce is sweet, mustardy, and the color of sunshine.

Prep: 20 minutes **Grill:** 35 minutes **Serves:** 4

4 boneless pork loin chops,
      cut 1 to 1¼ inches thick

Sauce

⅓ cup prepared mustard
⅓ cup red wine vinegar
4 teaspoons brown sugar
1 tablespoon butter or
      margarine
1 teaspoon Worcestershire
      sauce
½ teaspoon freshly ground
      black pepper
¼ to ½ teaspoon bottled hot
      pepper sauce

1 Trim fat from pork chops; set chops aside. For sauce, in a small saucepan whisk together the mustard, vinegar, brown sugar, butter, Worcestershire sauce, black pepper, and hot pepper sauce. Bring to boiling; reduce heat. Simmer, uncovered, for 5 minutes; remove from heat. Cool slightly. Divide sauce in half.

2 Preheat gas grill. Adjust for indirect cooking over medium heat (see page 5). Place chops on the grill rack over unlit burner. Cover and grill for 35 to 40 minutes or until an instant-read thermometer inserted in the center registers 160°, turning and brushing once with one portion of the sauce halfway through grilling. Serve the pork chops with remaining sauce.

Nutrition Facts per serving: 356 cal., 19 g total fat (6 g sat. fat), 107 mg chol., 379 mg sodium, 4 g carbo., 0 g fiber, 37 g pro.
Daily Values: 3% vit. A, 2% vit. C, 4% calcium, 10% iron

Jerk Pork ♥

In Jamaica, jerk—a special blend of herbs and spices—is smoked over the wood of the allspice tree. Grilling over hardwood chips would do the same for these chops (see tip, page 86).

Prep: 10 minutes **Marinate:** 2 hours **Grill:** 8 minutes **Serves:** 6

6 boneless pork loin chops, cut ¾ inch thick

Marinade

4 medium green onions, cut up

2 tablespoons cooking oil

1 tablespoon molasses

1 tablespoon rum

1 tablespoon lime juice

1 fresh jalapeño pepper, seeded and cut up

1 2-inch piece fresh ginger, cut up

2 large cloves garlic, cut up

¾ teaspoon ground allspice

½ teaspoon dried thyme, crushed

¼ teaspoon salt

1 Trim fat from pork chops. Place chops in a plastic bag set in a shallow dish: For marinade, in a blender container or food processor bowl combine green onions, cooking oil, molasses, rum, lime juice, jalapeño pepper, ginger, garlic, allspice, thyme, and salt. Cover and blend or process until nearly smooth. Pour over chops; seal bag. Marinate in the refrigerator for 2 to 24 hours, turning bag occasionally. Drain chops, discarding marinade.

2 Preheat gas grill. Reduce heat to medium. Place chops on the grill rack directly over heat. Cover and grill for 8 to 11 minutes or until an instant-read thermometer inserted in the center registers 160°, turning once halfway through grilling.

Nutrition Facts per serving: 174 cal., 8 g total fat (2 g sat. fat), 55 mg chol., 90 mg sodium, 3 g carbo., 0 g fiber, 20 g pro.
Daily Values: 1% vit. A, 5% vit. C, 3% calcium, 6% iron

Thai Pork Satay

Satay, an Indonesian snack food, gets main-course treatment in these tender pork skewers. Serve with steamed broccoli and rice or cucumber salad sprinkled with toasted sesame seeds.

Prep: 15 minutes **Marinate:** 2 hours **Grill:** 8 minutes **Serves:** 6

1½ pounds pork tenderloin or boneless pork loin roast

Marinade
- 2 tablespoons fish sauce
- 2 tablespoons lime juice
- 2 tablespoons finely chopped lemongrass or 1 teaspoon finely shredded lemon peel
- 1 tablespoon cooking oil
- 1 large clove garlic, minced

- 1 recipe Satay Sauce Chinese cabbage leaves

1 Trim fat from meat. Cut meat across the grain into ¼-inch-thick slices. If using loin roast, cut slices to make strips about 3 inches long and 1 inch wide. Place meat in a plastic bag set in a shallow dish. For marinade, in a small bowl combine fish sauce, lime juice, lemongrass, cooking oil, and garlic. Pour over meat; seal bag. Marinate in the refrigerator for 2 hours, turning bag occasionally.

2 Meanwhile, prepare Satay Sauce. Cover and refrigerate until ready to serve. Soak twelve 8-inch bamboo skewers in warm water for 1 to 2 hours. Drain bamboo skewers. Drain meat, discarding marinade. Thread meat onto skewers, accordion-style, leaving ¼-inch spaces between pieces.

3 Preheat gas grill. Reduce heat to medium. Place kabobs on the grill rack directly over heat. Cover and grill for 8 to 10 minutes or until meat is slightly pink in center, turning once halfway through grilling. Serve the kabobs on cabbage leaves with the sauce.

Satay Sauce: In a food processor bowl or blender container combine ¾ cup unsweetened coconut milk, ⅓ cup creamy peanut butter, 2 tablespoons lime juice, 2 tablespoons brown sugar, 2 tablespoons grated fresh ginger, 1 tablespoon fish sauce, and ½ teaspoon crushed red pepper or ¼ teaspoon ground red pepper. Cover and process or blend until smooth; transfer to a small bowl.

Nutrition Facts per serving: 333 cal., 19 g total fat (9 g sat. fat), 66 mg chol., 813 mg sodium, 9 g carbo., 2 g fiber, 32 g pro.
Daily Values: 8% vit. C, 3% calcium, 13% iron

Sweet and Spicy BBQ Ribs ♥

Americans like their barbecue sweet and spicy. Catsup kisses this homemade sauce with sweetness, and curry powder contributes some sass. If you don't have curry, use chili powder.

Prep: 35 minutes **Stand:** 30 minutes **Grill:** 1½ hours **Serves:** 8

Sauce

- 1½ cups catsup
- ¾ cup white wine vinegar
- ½ cup packed brown sugar
- 2 tablespoons curry powder
- 1 tablespoon Worcestershire sauce
- 2 or 3 cloves garlic, minced
- 1 teaspoon hickory-flavored salt
- 1 teaspoon pepper

- 3½ to 4 pounds pork loin back ribs

1 For sauce, in a medium bowl combine the catsup, vinegar, brown sugar, curry powder, Worcestershire sauce, garlic, hickory-flavored salt, and pepper. Cover and let stand at room temperature for 30 minutes or in the refrigerator for up to 5 days to blend flavors.

2 Preheat gas grill. Adjust for indirect cooking over medium heat (see page 5). Place ribs, bone side down, in a roasting pan; set the pan on the grill rack over unlit burner. Cover and grill for 1½ to 2 hours or until ribs are very tender, brushing generously with sauce the last 15 minutes of grilling. Cut ribs into serving-size pieces.

Nutrition Facts per serving: 295 cal., 8 g total fat (3 g sat. fat), 54 mg chol., 894 mg sodium, 27 g carbo., 1 g fiber, 26 g pro.
Daily Values: 5% vit. A, 13% vit. C, 4% calcium, 12% iron

are we grilling or barbecuing?

I love to barbecue—and I love to grill. Although "barbecue" used to refer to the act of gathering around a grill and cooking hot dogs and hamburgers, barbecuing and grilling may mean two different—though related—things.

Grilling means to cook food over direct heat. On a gas grill, it means to light the grill, place the food on the grill rack directly over the heat, and cook it at a high temperature. Barbecuing means to cook food slowly over low, indirect heat—often with flavorful smoke, sauces, and rubs. Bigger cuts of meat such as ribs, roasts, pork tenderloins, and whole birds are barbecued. Part of the fun of barbecue is that it tastes different in every part of the country.

Marilyn Cornelius
Test Kitchen Home Economist

Grilled Greek Leg of Lamb

Save this grilled leg of lamb for a leisurely Saturday evening—or don't. Sliced thin and quick-soaked in a lemon-oregano bath, it goes from ingredients to feast in a flash.

Prep: 20 minutes **Marinate:** 20 minutes **Grill:** 8 minutes **Serves:** 6

1½ to 2 pounds boneless leg
    of lamb
Marinade
  1 tablespoon finely
    shredded lemon peel
 ⅔ cup lemon juice
  6 tablespoons olive oil
 ⅓ cup snipped fresh oregano
 ½ teaspoon salt
 ⅛ teaspoon pepper

 ½ cup snipped fresh parsley
 ½ cup crumbled feta cheese
 ¼ cup sliced, pitted kalamata
    olives
 ¼ teaspoon ground
    cinnamon
 ¼ teaspoon pepper
  2 pounds plum tomatoes

1 Trim fat from meat. Cut meat across the grain into ½- to ¾-inch-thick slices. Place meat in a large bowl. For marinade, in a small bowl stir together the lemon peel, half of the lemon juice, 4 tablespoons of the oil, the oregano, salt, and the ⅛ teaspoon pepper. Pour marinade over lamb; cover and marinate at room temperature for 20 minutes, stirring once. (Or place meat in a plastic bag set in a shallow dish. Pour marinade over meat; seal bag. Marinate in the refrigerator for at least 8 hours or up to 24 hours, turning bag occasionally.)

2 Meanwhile, in a large bowl combine the remaining lemon juice, 1 tablespoon of the remaining oil, the parsley, feta cheese, olives, cinnamon, and the ¼ teaspoon pepper; set aside.

3 Drain meat, discarding marinade. Brush tomatoes with the remaining 1 tablespoon oil. Preheat gas grill. Reduce heat to medium-high. Place meat and tomatoes on the grill rack directly over heat. Cover and grill for 8 to 10 minutes or until meat is slightly pink in center and tomatoes are slightly charred, turning once halfway through grilling. Transfer tomatoes to cutting board; cool slightly and slice. Toss the tomatoes with the feta cheese mixture. Serve the meat with tomato mixture.

Nutrition Facts per serving: 256 cal., 14 g total fat (4 g sat. fat), 66 mg chol., 493 mg sodium, 11 g carbo., 0 g fiber, 22 g pro.
Daily Values: 15% vit. A, 80% vit. C, 6% calcium, 18% iron

Fragrant Minted Lamb Chops

Celebrate the arrival of the grilling season with the traditional springtime treat of lamb, given classic-with-a-twist treatment here in an aromatic mint-infused marinade.

Prep: 15 minutes   **Marinate:** 4 hours   **Grill:** 10 minutes   **Serves:** 4

8   lamb rib chops, cut 1 inch thick

Marinade

¼   cup snipped fresh mint
¼   cup lemon juice
2   tablespoons cooking oil
2   tablespoons water
1   tablespoon grated fresh ginger
1   large clove garlic, minced
1½   teaspoons paprika
1   teaspoon ground cumin
½   teaspoon salt
⅛   teaspoon ground red pepper

1   to 2 tablespoons finely shredded fresh mint
Rice pilaf (optional)
Fresh mint sprigs (optional)

1 Trim fat from lamb chops. Place chops in a plastic bag set in a shallow dish. For marinade, in a small bowl combine the snipped mint, the lemon juice, cooking oil, water, ginger, garlic, paprika, cumin, salt, and ground red pepper. Pour over chops; seal bag. Marinate in the refrigerator for 4 to 24 hours, turning bag occasionally. Drain chops, discarding marinade.

2 Preheat gas grill. Reduce heat to medium. Place chops on the grill rack directly over heat. Cover and grill until chops are desired doneness, turning once halfway through grilling. (Allow 10 to 14 minutes for medium rare or 14 to 16 minutes for medium.)

3 Transfer lamb chops to a serving platter; sprinkle with the shredded mint. If desired, serve the chops with rice pilaf and garnish with mint sprigs.

Nutrition Facts per serving: 210 cal., 12 g total fat (4 g sat. fat), 74 mg chol., 163 mg sodium, 1 g carbo., 0 g fiber, 23 g pro.
Daily Values: 3% vit. A, 8% vit. C, 2% calcium, 13% iron

Mongolian-Style Lamb Chops

Sesame oil comes two ways: toasted or Asian sesame oil, which is dark and strong and used to flavor foods—such as these lip-tingling lamb chops—and a light-colored version that's mild in flavor.

Prep: 15 minutes **Marinate:** 30 minutes **Grill:** 10 minutes **Serves:** 2 or 3

4 to 6 lamb loin chops,
    cut 1 inch thick

Marinade

2 tablespoons soy sauce
1 tablespoon brown sugar
6 cloves garlic, minced
1½ teaspoons grated fresh
    ginger
1 teaspoon toasted sesame
    oil

Fresh watercress sprigs
    (optional)
Lemon wedges (optional)

1 Trim fat from lamb chops. Place chops in a plastic bag set in a shallow dish. For marinade, in a small bowl stir together the soy sauce, brown sugar, garlic, ginger, and sesame oil. Pour over chops; seal bag. Marinate at room temperature for 30 minutes or in the refrigerator for 2 to 3 hours, turning bag occasionally. Drain chops, discarding marinade.

2 Preheat gas grill. Reduce heat to medium. Place chops on the grill rack directly over heat. Cover and grill until chops are desired doneness, turning once halfway through grilling. (Allow 10 to 14 minutes for medium rare or 14 to 16 minutes for medium.) If desired, garnish the chops with watercress sprigs and lemon wedges.

Nutrition Facts per serving: 450 cal., 20 g total fat (8 g sat. fat), 166 mg chol., 1158 mg sodium, 10 g carbo., 0 g fiber, 52 g pro.
Daily Values: 6% vit. C, 4% calcium, 34% iron

Mediterranean Veal Brochettes

"Brochette" is French for "skewer." Serve these tender veal brochettes over a Caesar salad or atop warm broken spaghetti tossed with fresh tarragon, olive oil, and sliced grilled vegetables.

Prep: 20 minutes **Marinate:** 1 hour **Grill:** 10 minutes **Serves:** 6

1½ pounds boneless veal or
    beef tenderloin,
    trimmed and cut into
    1½-inch cubes

Marinade

  3 green onions, sliced
 ¼ cup olive oil
  3 tablespoons lemon juice
  3 cloves garlic, minced
  2 teaspoons dried tarragon,
    crushed
 ½ teaspoon dried oregano,
    crushed
 ¼ teaspoon freshly ground
    black pepper

1 Place meat cubes in a plastic bag set in a shallow dish. For marinade, in a small bowl combine green onions, olive oil, lemon juice, garlic, tarragon, oregano, and pepper. Pour over meat; seal bag. Marinate in the refrigerator for 1 to 4 hours, turning bag occasionally. Drain meat, discarding marinade.

2 On six 12-inch metal skewers thread meat, leaving ¼-inch spaces between pieces. Preheat gas grill. Reduce heat to medium. Place kabobs on the grill rack directly over heat. Cover and grill for 10 to 12 minutes or until meat is slightly pink in center, turning occasionally to brown evenly.

Nutrition Facts per serving: 164 cal., 6 g total fat (1 g sat. fat), 88 mg chol., 62 mg sodium, 1 g carbo., 0 g fiber, 24 g pro.
Daily Values: 2% vit. C, 1% calcium, 5% iron

dinner on a stick

My family enjoys kebabs, brochettes, and skewered foods often. They're fun to eat and leave few dirty dishes behind (my favorite part!).

They do, however, take a little bit of extra preparation (outside of the cubing or chopping) and bear some watching on the grill. Metal skewers are easy to use. So are bamboo ones, though they need to be soaked in cold water for about 30 minutes before you thread them with food so they won't burn up on the grill.

Allow ¼-inch spaces between the chunks or cubes of food on the skewer to allow the heat to cook each piece evenly and thoroughly. When you think your food is nearly done, carefully cut into the largest meat chunk on the skewer to test for doneness.

Maryellen Krantz
Test Kitchen Home Economist

Poultry

Chicken Rolls with Apple Filling

In This Chapter:

Chicken and Citrus
    Salad 35
Chicken Rolls with Apple
    Filling 30
Chicken with Garlic
    and Basil 34
Finger-Lickin' Barbecue
    Chicken 28

Game Hens with Grilled
    Peppers 40
Greek Chicken Thighs 31
Grilled Turkey Piccata 37
Provençal Chicken and
    Pasta 32

Stuffed Turkey
    Tenderloins 38
Tandoori Chicken 29
Turkey with Cilantro
    Pesto 39

Finger-Lickin' Barbecue Chicken

Even if you're covered in sauce from ear to ear, you won't mind a bit. Something about good barbecued chicken makes a person perfectly content.

Prep: 45 minutes **Marinate:** 2 hours **Grill:** 50 minutes **Serves:** 6

3 to 4 pounds meaty chicken pieces (breasts, thighs, and drumsticks)

Marinade

1½ cups dry sherry
1 cup finely chopped onion
¼ cup lemon juice
6 cloves garlic, minced
2 bay leaves

Sauce

1 15-ounce can tomato puree
¼ cup honey
3 tablespoons molasses
1 teaspoon salt
½ teaspoon dried thyme, crushed
¼ to ½ teaspoon ground red pepper
¼ teaspoon black pepper
2 tablespoons white vinegar

1 Place chicken in a plastic bag set in a shallow dish. For marinade, in a medium bowl stir together sherry, onion, lemon juice, garlic, and bay leaves. Pour over chicken; seal bag. Marinate in the refrigerator for 2 to 4 hours, turning bag occasionally. Drain chicken, reserving marinade. Cover and refrigerate chicken until ready to grill.

2 For sauce, in a large saucepan combine the reserved marinade, the tomato puree, honey, molasses, salt, thyme, red pepper, and black pepper. Bring to boiling; reduce heat. Simmer, uncovered, about 30 minutes or until reduced to 2 cups. Remove from heat; remove bay leaves. Stir in vinegar.

3 Preheat gas grill. Adjust for indirect cooking over medium heat (see page 5). Place chicken, bone sides down, on the grill rack over unlit burner. Cover and grill for 50 to 60 minutes or until chicken is tender and no longer pink, brushing with some of the sauce the last 15 minutes of grilling. To serve, reheat the remaining sauce and pass with chicken.

Nutrition Facts per serving: 446 cal., 13 g total fat (4 g sat. fat), 104 mg chol., 735 mg sodium, 33 g carbo., 2 g fiber, 35 g pro.
Daily Values: 14% vit. A, 52% vit. C, 5% calcium, 20% iron

Tandoori Chicken

A half-chicken cooked in a real tandoor (a large clay oven) is done in less than five minutes in the intense 500°-plus heat. This grilled version takes a little longer but tastes every bit as delicious.

Prep: 15 minutes **Marinate:** 6 hours **Grill:** 50 minutes **Serves:** 4

2 to 2½ pounds meaty chicken pieces (breasts, thighs, and drumsticks)

Marinade

1 8-ounce carton plain yogurt

4 teaspoons lemon juice

2 teaspoons paprika

1½ teaspoons grated fresh ginger

1 clove garlic, minced

½ teaspoon ground coriander

¼ teaspoon salt

¼ teaspoon ground cumin

¼ teaspoon ground turmeric

⅛ to ¼ teaspoon ground red pepper

Chutney (optional)

1 If desired, remove skin from chicken. Place chicken in a plastic bag set in a shallow dish. For marinade, in a medium bowl combine yogurt, lemon juice, paprika, ginger, garlic, coriander, salt, cumin, turmeric, and red pepper. Pour over chicken; seal bag. Marinate in the refrigerator for 6 to 24 hours, turning bag occasionally.

2 Drain chicken, reserving marinade. Cover and refrigerate the marinade until needed.

3 Preheat gas grill. Adjust for indirect cooking over medium heat (see page 5). Place chicken, bone sides down, on the grill rack over unlit burner. Cover and grill for 50 to 60 minutes or until chicken is tender and no longer pink, brushing twice with marinade during the first half of grilling and turning once halfway through grilling. If desired, serve chicken with chutney.

Nutrition Facts per serving: 301 cal., 14 g total fat (4 g sat. fat), 107 mg chol., 278 mg sodium, 6 g carbo., 1 g fiber, 37 g pro.
Daily Values: 14% vit. A, 7% vit. C, 13% calcium, 10% iron

perfectly safe poultry

The key to feeling confident about cooking and eating poultry is simple: Keep it clean. Follow these few safety guidelines for handling fresh poultry and you'll never have a worry:

● Wash your hands, work surfaces, and utensils in hot, soapy water after handling raw poultry to prevent spreading bacteria to other foods.

● Use a plastic cutting board to cut raw poultry; it's easier to clean and disinfect than a wooden one.

● Never use the same plate to transfer uncooked and cooked poultry to and from the grill.

Chicken Rolls with Apple Filling

Great any time of year—but a perfect way to celebrate a beautiful fall day—these pretty chicken bundles are full of autumnal flavors.

Prep: 25 minutes **Grill:** 12 minutes **Serves:** 4

4 medium skinless, boneless chicken breast halves (about 1 pound total)

Filling

4 ounces reduced-fat bulk pork sausage

¼ cup coarsely shredded apple

1 tablespoon snipped fresh parsley

Glaze

⅓ cup apple jelly

¼ teaspoon dried sage, crushed

2 medium red and/or green cooking apples, cut crosswise into ½-inch slices

1 Place a piece of chicken between 2 pieces of heavy plastic wrap. Using the flat side of a meat mallet, pound the chicken lightly into a rectangle about ⅛ inch thick. Remove plastic wrap. Repeat with remaining chicken pieces.

2 For filling, in a small bowl combine the sausage, shredded apple, and parsley. Place one-fourth of the filling on each chicken piece, spreading almost to the edges. Starting from a narrow end, roll up into a spiral; secure with wooden toothpicks.* For glaze, stir apple jelly until smooth; stir in sage.

3 Preheat gas grill. Reduce heat to medium. Place chicken on the grill rack directly over heat. Cover and grill for 12 to 15 minutes or until chicken is tender and no longer pink, turning and brushing once with glaze halfway through grilling.

4 While the chicken is grilling, add apple slices to grill. Cover and grill about 5 minutes or until apples are tender and slightly charred, turning and brushing once with glaze halfway through grilling. Serve the chicken with apples.

Nutrition Facts per serving: 272 cal., 3 g total fat (1 g sat. fat), 78 mg chol., 281 mg sodium, 31 g carbo., 2 g fiber, 31 g pro.
Daily Values: 2% vit. A, 10% vit. C, 2% calcium, 5% iron

*Note: If you like, wrap the chicken rolls and refrigerate for up to 4 hours before grilling. You may need to add an extra couple of minutes to the grilling time.

Greek Chicken Thighs

Chicken thighs are an oft-overlooked cut. They're a good dark-meat alternative to breasts—and usually less expensive too. Serve these with orzo and a cucumber-tomato salad.

Prep: 20 minutes **Marinate:** 30 minutes **Grill:** 30 minutes **Serves:** 4 to 6

8 chicken thighs (about
   2½ pounds total)

Marinade

¼ cup dry red wine
2 tablespoons olive oil
2 tablespoons finely
   chopped red onion
1 teaspoon finely shredded
   lemon peel
1 teaspoon snipped fresh
   rosemary
1 teaspoon snipped fresh
   oregano
1 clove garlic, minced
¼ teaspoon salt
¼ teaspoon pepper

½ cup crumbled basil- and
   tomato-flavored feta
   cheese or plain feta
   cheese

1 Remove skin from chicken. Place chicken in a plastic bag set in a shallow dish. For marinade, in a small bowl combine the red wine, olive oil, onion, lemon peel, rosemary, oregano, garlic, salt, and pepper. Pour over chicken; seal bag. Marinate at room temperature for 30 minutes or in the refrigerator for 4 to 24 hours, turning bag occasionally. Drain chicken, reserving marinade.

2 Preheat gas grill. Reduce heat to medium. Place chicken on the grill rack directly over heat. Cover and grill for 30 to 35 minutes or until chicken is tender and no longer pink, turning and brushing once with marinade halfway through grilling.

3 Sprinkle the chicken with feta cheese. Cover loosely with foil and let stand for 2 minutes before serving.

Nutrition Facts per serving: 389 cal., 19 g total fat (6 g sat. fat), 205 mg chol., 512 mg sodium, 2 g carbo., 0 g fiber, 47 g pro.
Daily Values: 4% vit. A, 11% vit. C, 12% calcium, 13% iron

Provençal Chicken and Pasta

The sunlight has a certain quality in the south of France, and the flavors of its food do too: fruity olive oil, lots of fresh vegetables, and the generous use of herbs.

Prep: 20 minutes **Grill:** 12 minutes **Serves:** 4

8 ounces dried plain penne pasta or tomato- or garlic-and-herb-flavored penne pasta

4 medium skinless, boneless chicken breast halves (about 1 pound total)

1 medium zucchini, halved lengthwise

8 thick asparagus spears (8 to 10 ounces total), trimmed

3 tablespoons olive oil

1 tablespoon dried fines herbes or herbes de Provence, crushed

½ teaspoon salt

1 tablespoon snipped fresh thyme

½ cup finely shredded Romano cheese

1 Cook pasta according to package directions. Meanwhile, brush chicken, zucchini, and asparagus with 1 tablespoon of the oil; sprinkle all sides with fines herbes and salt.

2 Preheat gas grill. Reduce heat to medium. Place chicken, zucchini, and asparagus on the grill rack directly over heat. Cover and grill for 12 to 15 minutes or until chicken is tender and no longer pink and vegetables are tender, turning once halfway through grilling.

3 Transfer chicken and vegetables to cutting board; cool slightly. Cut chicken and zucchini into 1-inch cubes; slice asparagus into 1-inch pieces. Drain pasta; return to saucepan. Add chicken, vegetables, the remaining oil, and thyme; toss well. Sprinkle each serving with Romano cheese and season to taste with pepper.

Nutrition Facts per serving: 480 cal., 17 g total fat (2 g sat. fat), 69 mg chol., 492 mg sodium, 45 g carbo., 4 g fiber, 35 g pro.
Daily Values: 7% vit. A, 20% vit. C, 15% calcium, 17% iron

culinary cousins

Fines herbes and herbes de Provence—both French herb blends—are interchangeable. Fines herbes is a quartet of chervil, chives, parsley, and tarragon. Herbes de Provence is a mélange of basil, fennel, lavender, marjoram, rosemary, sage, savory, and thyme.

Chicken with Garlic and Basil

Cooking a whole chicken with lemon in the cavity imparts a mouthwatering aroma and light citrus flavor to the meat and makes it juicy and tender.

Prep: 20 minutes   **Grill:** 1¼ hours   **Stand:** 10 minutes   **Serves:** 5

1   3- to 3½-pound whole broiler-fryer chicken
4   cloves garlic, peeled
½   lemon, sliced
1   tablespoon snipped fresh basil or 1 teaspoon dried basil, crushed
⅛   teaspoon salt
1   tablespoon olive oil or cooking oil
1   tablespoon lemon juice
    Fresh oregano sprigs (optional)

1 Remove neck and giblets from chicken. Twist wing tips under back. Cut 2 of the garlic cloves in half lengthwise. Rub skin of chicken with cut garlic. Place garlic halves and lemon slices in cavity of chicken. Mince remaining 2 garlic cloves. Combine minced garlic, basil, and salt; set aside. Starting at the neck on one side of breast, slip your fingers between skin and meat, loosening skin as you work toward the tail. Once your entire hand is under the skin, free the skin around the thigh and leg up to, but not around, the tips of the drumsticks. Repeat on other side. Rub basil mixture over surface under skin. Fasten opening with toothpicks. Combine oil and lemon juice; brush over chicken.

2 Preheat gas grill. Adjust for indirect cooking over medium heat (see page 5). Place chicken, breast side up, on a rack in a roasting pan; set pan on the grill rack over unlit burner. Cover and grill for 1¼ to 1¾ hours or until chicken is no longer pink, the drumsticks move easily in their sockets, and an instant-read thermometer inserted into the inside thigh muscle registers 180°, brushing occasionally with oil mixture up to the last 5 minutes of grilling. Remove chicken. Cover with foil; let stand for 10 minutes before carving. If desired, garnish with oregano.

Nutrition Facts per serving: 283 cal., 17 g total fat (4 g sat. fat), 94 mg chol., 146 mg sodium, 1 g carbo., 0 g fiber, 29 g pro.
Daily Values: 5% vit. C, 2% calcium, 8% iron

Chicken and Citrus Salad ♥

This Florida-style chicken salad is freshened up with the citrus that made the Sunshine State famous. Serve it with warm corn bread and iced fruit tea.

Prep: 15 minutes **Grill:** 12 minutes **Serves:** 4

Dressing

⅔ cup bottled fat-free honey Dijon salad dressing

1½ teaspoons finely shredded lime peel

1 tablespoon lime juice

4 medium skinless, boneless chicken breast halves (about 1 pound total)
Salt and pepper
Nonstick cooking spray

1 medium grapefruit, peeled and cut into ½-inch slices

2 medium oranges, peeled and cut into ½-inch slices

6 cups torn romaine lettuce or mixed salad greens

1 For dressing, in a small bowl combine salad dressing, lime peel, and lime juice. Set aside 2 tablespoons of the dressing. Cover and refrigerate the remaining dressing until ready to serve.

2 Sprinkle chicken lightly with salt and pepper. Brush both sides of chicken with the reserved 2 tablespoons dressing.

3 Preheat gas grill. Reduce heat to medium. Place chicken on the grill rack directly over heat. Cover and grill for 12 to 15 minutes or until chicken is tender and no longer pink, turning once halfway through grilling.

4 While the chicken is grilling, lightly coat a grill tray with cooking spray. Place grapefruit and oranges on grill tray; add to grill. Cover and grill about 4 minutes or until grapefruit and oranges are heated through, turning once halfway through grilling.

5 Transfer chicken and fruit to cutting board. Cut chicken diagonally into thin slices. Coarsely chop grapefruit and quarter orange slices. Divide romaine among 4 dinner plates. Arrange warm chicken and fruit on top of romaine. Drizzle with the remaining dressing.

Nutrition Facts per serving: 229 cal., 2 g total fat (0 g sat. fat), 66 mg chol., 519 mg sodium, 24 g carbo., 4 g fiber, 29 g pro.
Daily Values: 48% vit. A, 103% vit. C, 6% calcium, 10% iron

grill gadgetry

Nonstick enamel-coated grill trays, woks, and pizza pans come in all sizes and are perforated with holes to allow heat and smoke to cook and flavor foods. Grill baskets are great for grilling vegetables, fish, and seafood that might otherwise fall through the grate.

One of the most useful accessories for a gas grill is a second gas tank. You'll never again have to worry that you'll run out of fire midway through meal preparation.

Grilled Turkey Piccata ♥

A dish done piccata-style always has lemon, parsley, and capers in it. Try making this Italian specialty with boneless chicken breasts in place of the turkey tenderloin steaks.

Prep: 15 minutes **Grill:** 12 minutes **Serves:** 4

2 lemons

Rub

4 teaspoons olive oil
2 teaspoons snipped fresh
   rosemary or ½ teaspoon
   dried rosemary, crushed
¼ teaspoon salt
¼ teaspoon freshly ground
   black pepper

4 ½-inch-thick turkey breast
   tenderloin steaks (about
   1¼ to 1½ pounds total)
1 tablespoon drained capers
1 tablespoon snipped fresh
   Italian flat-leaf parsley

1 Finely shred enough peel from one of the lemons to make 1 teaspoon; set aside. Halve and squeeze the juice from that lemon (should have about 3 tablespoons); set aside. Cut the other lemon into very thin slices; set aside.

2 For rub, in a small bowl combine the shredded lemon peel, 2 teaspoons of the olive oil, the rosemary, salt, and pepper. Sprinkle the mixture evenly over both sides of turkey steaks; rub in with your fingers.

3 Preheat gas grill. Reduce heat to medium. Place turkey on the grill rack directly over heat. Cover and grill for 6 minutes. Turn turkey. Arrange lemon slices on top of turkey, overlapping if necessary. Cover and grill for 6 to 9 minutes more or until turkey is tender and no longer pink.

4 Meanwhile, in a small saucepan combine the remaining olive oil, the lemon juice, and the capers. Heat through.

5 Remove turkey steaks to a serving platter. Drizzle with the warm caper mixture. Sprinkle with parsley.

Nutrition Facts per serving: 159 cal., 5 g total fat (1 g sat. fat), 71 mg chol., 269 mg sodium, 1 g carbo., 0 g fiber, 26 g pro.
Daily Values: 1% vit. A, 12% vit. C, 1% calcium, 8% iron

make your own steak

Turkey steaks appear often on the table at my house. They're meaty and substantial but lighter than beef steak. If you can't find turkey tenderloin steaks at your local grocery store, buy whole turkey tenderloins; then cut them horizontally into ½-inch-thick slices.

Lori Wilson
Test Kitchen Home Economist

Stuffed Turkey Tenderloins

Stuffing and cooking a turkey was never so fast. Instead of bread, though, these turkey tenderloins go garden-style with a melt-in-your-mouth spinach and cheese filling.

Prep: 15 minutes **Grill:** 16 minutes **Serves:** 4

2 8-ounce turkey breast
    tenderloins

Filling
2 cups chopped fresh
    spinach leaves
3 ounces semisoft goat
    cheese (chèvre) or feta
    cheese, crumbled
    (about ¾ cup)
½ teaspoon black pepper

1 tablespoon olive oil
1 teaspoon paprika
½ teaspoon salt
⅛ to ¼ teaspoon ground red
    pepper

1 Make a pocket in each turkey tenderloin by cutting lengthwise from one side almost to, but not through, the opposite side; set aside. For filling, in a medium bowl combine the spinach, cheese, and black pepper. Spoon the filling into the pockets. Tie the turkey with 100-percent-cotton string in 3 or 4 places to hold in the filling.

2 In a small bowl combine the oil, paprika, salt, and red pepper; brush evenly over turkey tenderloins.

3 Preheat gas grill. Reduce heat to medium. Place turkey on the grill rack directly over heat. Cover and grill for 16 to 20 minutes or until turkey is tender and no longer pink in center of the thickest part, turning once halfway through grilling. Remove and discard strings; slice turkey crosswise.

Nutrition Facts per serving: 220 cal., 12 g total fat (4 g sat. fat), 68 mg chol., 458 mg sodium, 1 g carbo., 1 g fiber, 26 g pro.
Daily Values: 24% vit. A, 14% vit. C, 5% calcium, 13% iron

Turkey with Cilantro Pesto

Cilantro and buttery cashews are a nice change of pace in this pesto, where it does delicious double duty as both a rub for the turkey tenderloins and a savory sauce for the accompanying pasta.

Prep: 25 minutes   **Grill:** 25 minutes   **Serves:** 6

Pesto

- 1 cup firmly packed fresh cilantro leaves
- ½ cup firmly packed fresh Italian flat-leaf parsley leaves
- ½ cup grated Parmesan cheese
- ½ cup salted cashews
- 1 small clove garlic, quartered
- ¼ cup olive oil or cooking oil

- 2 8-ounce turkey breast tenderloins
- 12 ounces dried fettuccine or linguine
  Fresh cilantro sprigs

1 For pesto, in a blender container or food processor bowl combine the 1 cup cilantro, the parsley, Parmesan cheese, ¼ cup of the cashews, and the garlic. Cover and blend or process with several on-off turns until a paste forms, stopping the machine several times and scraping the sides. With the machine running, gradually add the oil and blend or process until the consistency of soft butter. Rub both sides of turkey tenderloins with about 2 tablespoons of the pesto.

2 Preheat gas grill. Adjust for indirect cooking over medium heat (see page 5). Place turkey on the grill rack over unlit burner. Cover and grill for 25 to 30 minutes or until turkey is tender and no longer pink in center of the thickest part.

3 Meanwhile, cook pasta according to package directions. Drain pasta; return to saucepan. Add the remaining pesto and the remaining cashews; toss well. Divide the pasta mixture among 6 dinner plates. Thinly slice turkey and arrange on top of pasta mixture. Garnish with cilantro sprigs.

Nutrition Facts per serving: 483 cal., 18 g total fat (4 g sat. fat), 53 mg chol., 197 mg sodium, 47 g carbo., 2 g fiber, 31 g pro.
Daily Values: 22% vit. A, 19% vit. C, 16% calcium, 21% iron

Game Hens with Grilled Peppers

Cutting the Cornish hens in half accomplishes two things: It allows them to cook much faster than they would whole, and makes two servings of one bird (which is just enough).

Prep: 25 minutes **Grill:** 40 minutes **Serves:** 4

2 1½-pound Cornish game hens

Cumin Butter

¼ cup butter or margarine, melted

½ teaspoon salt

½ teaspoon freshly ground black pepper

½ teaspoon ground cumin

3 red, yellow, and/or green sweet peppers, quartered

1 ancho pepper, quartered

1 medium red onion, cut into ½-inch slices

1 Using kitchen shears or a long heavy knife, cut game hens in half. Twist wing tips under back. For cumin butter, in a small bowl combine melted butter, salt, pepper, and cumin. Divide mixture in half. Use one portion to brush over both sides of hens. Set the other portion aside.

2 Preheat gas grill. Adjust for indirect cooking over medium heat (see page 5). Place hens, bone sides down, on the grill rack over unlit burner. Cover and grill for 40 to 50 minutes or until hens are tender and no longer pink.

3 While the hens are grilling, brush the sweet peppers, ancho pepper, and onion with the remaining butter mixture; add peppers and onion to grill. If vegetables are over medium-high heat, cover and grill about 10 minutes or until tender and slightly charred, turning once halfway through grilling. If vegetables are over medium heat, cover and grill about 20 minutes or until tender and slightly charred, turning once halfway through grilling.

4 Remove hens and vegetables from grill; keep hens warm. Cut peppers into strips; chop onion. Toss together peppers and onion. To serve, divide pepper mixture among 4 dinner plates. Arrange hens on top of pepper mixture.

Nutrition Facts per serving: 493 cal., 35 g total fat (13 g sat. fat), 153 mg chol., 509 mg sodium, 9 g carbo., 2 g fiber, 38 g pro.
Daily Values: 31% vit. A, 285% vit. C, 2% calcium, 4% iron

Fish & Seafood

Lobster Tails with Chive Butter

In This Chapter:

Fish and Vegetable
    Packets 47
Fish with Orange-Basil
    Salsa 49
Grilled Mussels with Garlic
    Butter 52

Grilled Tuna Niçoise
    Salad 44
Lime-Marinated Halibut 43
Lobster Tails with Chive
    Butter 51
Red Snapper with Herb-
    Pecan Crust 46

Seafood Skewers with
    Peanut Sauce 50
Sesame-Ginger Grilled
    Salmon 42
Wasabi-Glazed
    Whitefish 48

Sesame-Ginger Grilled Salmon

Toasting sesame seeds is easy. Place them in a small, heavy skillet over low heat and cook, stirring frequently, until they're golden brown and fragrant, about 5 to 7 minutes.

Prep: 15 minutes **Marinate:** 30 minutes **Grill:** 22 minutes **Serves:** 4

4 5-ounce fresh skinless salmon fillets, ¾ to 1 inch thick

Marinade

¼ cup light soy sauce
2 tablespoons lime juice
1 tablespoon grated fresh ginger
1 teaspoon brown sugar
½ teaspoon toasted sesame oil

2 tablespoons sesame seeds, toasted

1 Rinse fish; pat dry with paper towels. For marinade, in a shallow dish combine soy sauce, lime juice, ginger, brown sugar, and sesame oil. Add fish, turning to coat. Cover and marinate at room temperature for 30 minutes or in the refrigerator for 2 hours, turning fish occasionally. Drain fish, discarding marinade.

2 Lightly grease the rack of a gas grill. Preheat grill. Adjust for indirect cooking over medium heat (see page 5). Place fish on the grill rack over unlit burner, tucking under any thin edges.

3 Sprinkle the fish with sesame seed. Cover and grill until fish just flakes easily when tested with a fork. (Allow 15 to 18 minutes per ½-inch thickness of fish.) Do not turn.

Nutrition Facts per serving: 282 cal., 17 g total fat (4 g sat. fat), 93 mg chol., 130 mg sodium, 2 g carbo., 1 g fiber, 29 g pro.
Daily Values: 12% vit. A, 8% vit. C, 8% calcium, 9% iron

mmm, it's marinated

Marinating a piece of meat or poultry makes it taste great. It also makes it tender and juicy.

In general, a marinade has three elements: an acid, such as wine, vinegar, or lemon juice; seasonings, such as garlic, herbs, and hot peppers; and an oil, often cooking or olive oil. The seasonings make the meat or poultry flavorful (and the oil, too, if it's a fruity olive oil or other flavored oil), and the acid breaks it down until it's melt-in-your-mouth tender. Remember: If a recipe calls for leftover marinade to be served with the grilled food, it must be boiled to destroy any harmful bacteria from the raw meat, poultry, or fish. It will look more attractive if you strain it before serving.

Lime-Marinated Halibut ♥

The lime juice in this marinade flavors and tenderizes the fish—but don't let it soak any longer than about 20 minutes or the acid will begin to affect its appearance, turning it white or opaque.

Prep: 8 minutes **Marinate:** 20 minutes **Grill:** 8 minutes **Serves:** 4

4 5-ounce fresh halibut
   steaks, cut 1 inch thick

Marinade

1 lime
2 teaspoons olive oil
¼ teaspoon salt

Tomato-Herb Couscous

1¼ cups chicken broth
1 cup quick-cooking
   couscous
1 cup cherry tomatoes,
   halved
2 tablespoons snipped fresh
   cilantro
2 tablespoons snipped fresh
   mint

1 Rinse fish; pat dry with paper towels. Finely shred enough peel from the lime to make 1 teaspoon; set aside. For marinade, halve and squeeze enough juice from the lime to make 2 tablespoons. In a shallow dish combine the lime juice, olive oil, and salt. Add fish, turning to coat. Cover and marinate at room temperature for 20 minutes, turning fish once. Drain fish, discarding marinade.

2 Lightly grease the rack of a gas grill. Preheat grill. Reduce heat to medium. Place fish on the grill rack directly over heat. Cover and grill for 8 to 12 minutes or until fish just flakes easily when tested with a fork, gently turning once halfway through grilling.

3 Meanwhile, for couscous, in a saucepan bring chicken broth to boiling. Stir in couscous. Remove from heat; cover and let stand for 5 minutes. Fluff with a fork and stir in cherry tomatoes, cilantro, mint, and the reserved lime peel. Cover and let stand for 2 to 3 minutes more or until tomatoes are warm. Serve the fish with Tomato-Herb Couscous.

Nutrition Facts per serving: 372 cal., 7 g total fat (1 g sat. fat), 45 mg chol., 545 mg sodium, 39 g carbo., 3 g fiber, 37 g pro.
Daily Values: 13% vit. A, 25% vit. C, 9% calcium, 14% iron

Grilled Tuna Niçoise Salad

For company-quality presentation, arrange this classic south-of-France salad on one large platter. Accompany it with crusty French bread and sparkling water or white wine.

Prep: 30 minutes **Marinate:** 20 minutes **Grill:** 10 minutes **Serves:** 6

1 pound fresh tuna steaks, cut 1 inch thick

1 recipe Balsamic Vinaigrette

1½ pounds red-skinned potatoes, cut into ¼-inch slices

8 ounces green beans, trimmed

2 tablespoons olive oil

6 cups sliced romaine lettuce

1 cup cherry tomatoes, halved

½ cup pitted kalamata olives

¼ cup thinly sliced red onion

2 hard-cooked eggs, cut into wedges

2 teaspoons snipped fresh tarragon

1 Rinse fish; pat dry with paper towels. Place fish in a shallow dish; set aside. Prepare Balsamic Vinaigrette. Pour ¼ cup of the vinaigrette over fish, turning to coat. Cover and marinate at room temperature for 20 minutes, turning fish once. Drain fish, discarding marinade.

2 Meanwhile, in a saucepan cook potatoes in a small amount of boiling salted water for 10 minutes, adding green beans for the last 3 minutes of cooking. Drain and cool slightly. Place potatoes and beans in a bowl and toss with olive oil. Spread vegetables in a single layer in a grill basket.

3 Lightly grease the rack of a gas grill. Preheat grill. Reduce heat to medium. Place fish and basket of vegetables on the grill rack directly over heat. Cover and grill until fish just flakes easily when tested with a fork and vegetables are tender, turning once halfway through grilling. (Allow 8 to 12 minutes for fish and about 10 minutes for vegetables.) Remove from grill. Cut fish diagonally into ¼-inch slices.

4 In a large bowl toss together romaine, cherry tomatoes, olives, and red onion. Divide among 4 dinner plates. Arrange the fish, potatoes, beans, and eggs on top of romaine mixture. Drizzle with the remaining vinaigrette. Sprinkle with tarragon.

Balsamic Vinaigrette: In a screw-top jar combine ⅓ cup balsamic vinegar or red wine vinegar, ¼ cup olive oil, 1 tablespoon Dijon-style mustard, and ½ teaspoon bottled minced garlic; cover and shake well. Season to taste with sugar, salt, and pepper. Makes about ¾ cup dressing.

Nutrition Facts per serving: 416 cal., 22 g total fat (4 g sat. fat), 135 mg chol., 264 mg sodium, 29 g carbo., 5 g fiber, 26 g pro.
Daily Values: 71% vit. A, 68% vit. C, 7% calcium, 19% iron

Red Snapper with Herb-Pecan Crust

Chopped pecans make for a toasty, Southern-style crust on this grilled red snapper. Serve it with warm corn bread and turnip or collard greens cooked with a little bacon.

Prep: 15 minutes **Grill:** 6 minutes **Serves:** 4

4 5- to 6-ounce fresh red snapper fillets with skin, ¾ to 1 inch thick

Topping
⅓ cup finely chopped pecans
2 tablespoons fine dry bread crumbs
2 tablespoons butter or margarine, softened
1 tablespoon snipped fresh Italian flat-leaf parsley
2 garlic cloves, minced
1 teaspoon finely shredded lemon peel
¼ teaspoon salt
⅛ teaspoon black pepper
    Dash ground red pepper

    Snipped fresh Italian flat-leaf parsley
    Lemon wedges (optional)

1 Rinse fish; pat dry with paper towels. Set aside. For topping, in a small bowl combine pecans, bread crumbs, butter, parsley, garlic, lemon peel, salt, black pepper, and red pepper.

2 Lightly grease the rack of a gas grill. Preheat grill. Reduce heat to medium. Place fish, skin side down, on the grill rack directly over heat. Spoon topping on top of fish; spread slightly.

3 Cover and grill until fish just flakes easily when tested with a fork. (Allow 4 to 6 minutes per ½-inch thickness of fish.) Using a wide spatula, transfer fish to a serving platter. Sprinkle with additional snipped parsley and, if desired, serve with fresh lemon wedges.

Nutrition Facts per serving: 268 cal., 14 g total fat (2 g sat. fat), 52 mg chol., 287 mg sodium, 7 g carbo., 8 g fiber, 30 g pro.
Daily Values: 7% vit. A, 4% vit. C, 4% calcium, 4% iron

is it done yet?

Fish on the grill is one of my favorites, but testing for doneness can be difficult. Because fish cooks quickly, it has to be watched so it doesn't dry out—but you obviously don't want it undercooked either. Here's how to tell when fish is ready to eat: Grill it just until the flesh is opaque through the thickest part. (Don't cook it until it's dry, because it will be tough.) Then give it the fork test: Poke a fork into the thickest part of the fish; then gently twist the fork and pull up some of the flesh. If it's done, the fish will flake easily.

Kay Springer
Test Kitchen Home Economist

Fish and Vegetable Packets

The whole meal—except for the accompanying rice—is cooked on the grill in a foil packet. Served in its foil pouch, it makes an attractive, great-tasting dinner with few dishes to wash.

Prep: 40 minutes **Grill:** 12 minutes **Serves:** 4

1 pound fresh or frozen skinless salmon, orange roughy, cod, or tilapia fillets, ½ to ¾ inch thick
Nonstick cooking spray

Vegetables

2 cups carrots, cut into thin bite-size strips

2 cups red sweet pepper, cut into thin, bite-size strips

12 medium asparagus spears (about 12 ounces), trimmed

4 small yellow summer squash (about 1 pound), cut into ¼-inch slices

Seasonings

½ cup dry white wine or chicken broth

2 teaspoons snipped fresh rosemary or ½ teaspoon dried rosemary, crushed

2 cloves garlic, minced

¼ teaspoon salt

¼ teaspoon black pepper

2 tablespoons butter or margarine, cut up

Hot cooked white or brown rice

1 Thaw fish, if frozen. Rinse fish; pat dry with paper towels. Cut into 4 serving-size pieces. Set aside.

2 Cut eight 18×18-inch pieces of heavy foil. Place 2 sheets together to form 4 stacks. Coat one side of each stack with cooking spray. For vegetables, divide carrots, sweet pepper, and asparagus among stacks of foil. Top with the fish and squash.

3 For seasonings, in a small bowl combine wine, rosemary, garlic, salt, and black pepper. Drizzle over fish and vegetables; dot with butter. Bring up 2 opposite edges of foil and seal with a double fold. Fold remaining ends to completely enclose the fish and vegetables, leaving space for steam to build.

4 Preheat gas grill. Reduce heat to medium. Place foil packets on the grill rack directly over heat. Cover and grill until fish just flakes easily when tested with a fork and vegetables are crisp-tender.* (Allow 12 to 14 minutes per ½-inch thickness of fish.) Serve with hot cooked rice.

Nutrition Facts per serving: 518 cal., 22 g total fat (8 g sat. fat), 91 mg chol., 294 mg sodium, 43 g carbo., 6 g fiber, 32 g pro.
Daily Values: 208% vit. A, 207% vit. C, 15% calcium, 22% iron

*****Note:** When checking for doneness, open the packets carefully to avoid burns from hot steam.

Wasabi-Glazed Whitefish ♥

Wasabi—the head-clearing green condiment traditionally served with sushi—adds a subtle fire to this fish dish. Look for wasabi powder or paste in Japanese markets or larger supermarkets.

Prep: 15 minutes **Grill:** 8 minutes **Serves:** 4

2 tablespoons light soy sauce

1 teaspoon toasted sesame oil

½ teaspoon sugar

¼ teaspoon wasabi powder or 1 tablespoon prepared horseradish

4 4-ounce fresh skinless whitefish, sea bass, or orange roughy fillets, 1 inch thick

Slaw

1 medium zucchini, coarsely shredded (about 1⅓ cups)

1 cup sliced radishes

1 cup fresh pea pods

2 tablespoons snipped fresh chives

3 tablespoons rice vinegar

1 Combine soy sauce, ½ teaspoon of the sesame oil, ¼ teaspoon of the sugar, and the wasabi powder. Rinse fish; pat dry with paper towels. Brush both sides of fish with soy mixture.

2 Lightly grease the rack of a gas grill. Preheat grill. Reduce heat to medium. Place fish on the grill rack directly over heat, tucking under any thin edges. Cover and grill for 8 to 12 minutes or until fish just flakes easily when tested with a fork, gently turning once halfway through grilling.

3 Meanwhile, for slaw, in a medium bowl combine the zucchini, radishes, pea pods, and chives. Stir together vinegar, the remaining sesame oil, and the remaining sugar. Drizzle over the zucchini mixture; toss to coat. Serve the fish with slaw.

Nutrition Facts per serving: 141 cal., 3 g total fat (1 g sat. fat), 60 mg chol., 363 mg sodium, 6 g carbo., 1 g fiber, 24 g pro.
Daily Values: 3% vit. A, 46% vit. C, 3% calcium, 10% iron

Fish with Orange-Basil Salsa

Any sort of fish—salmon, halibut, swordfish, or shark—works well in this quick-to-fix dish. Make the refreshing salsa while the fish marinates in the refrigerator.

Prep: 15 minutes **Marinate:** 1 hour **Grill:** 6 minutes **Serves:** 4

4 4- to 6-ounce fresh
   salmon, halibut,
   swordfish, or shark
   steaks, cut ¾ inch thick
1 tablespoon olive oil
1 recipe Southeast Asian
   Marinade or Herb-
   Lemon Marinade

Salsa
1 teaspoon finely shredded
   orange peel
2 oranges, peeled, sectioned,
   and chopped (1 cup), or
   one 11-ounce can
   mandarin orange
   sections, drained
¼ cup snipped fresh basil or
   mint
¼ cup finely chopped red
   onion
   Dash salt

1 Rinse fish; pat dry with paper towels. Brush both sides of fish with oil. Place fish in a plastic bag set in a shallow dish. Prepare the Southeast Asian Marinade or Herb-Lemon Marinade. Pour over fish; seal bag. Marinate in the refrigerator for 1 hour, turning bag once. Drain fish, discarding marinade.

2 Meanwhile, for salsa, in a bowl combine orange peel, oranges, basil, red onion, and salt. Cover and refrigerate until ready to serve. If desired, bring to room temperature before serving.

3 Lightly grease the rack of a gas grill. Preheat grill. Reduce heat to medium. Place fish on the grill rack directly over heat. Cover and grill for 6 to 9 minutes or until fish just flakes easily when tested with a fork, gently turning once halfway through grilling. Serve the fish with salsa.

Southeast Asian Marinade: In a small saucepan cook 3 tablespoons chopped fresh jalapeño pepper and 1 clove garlic, minced, in 1 tablespoon cooking oil over medium heat until tender. Transfer to a food processor bowl. Add ¼ cup lime or lemon juice, 2 tablespoons soy sauce, and 1 tablespoon chopped, peeled fresh ginger. Cover and process until smooth.

Herb-Lemon Marinade: In a small bowl combine 3 tablespoons olive oil; 3 tablespoon water or dry white wine; 1 teaspoon finely shredded lemon peel; 3 tablespoons lemon juice; 3 cloves garlic, minced; 2 teaspoons dried thyme, rosemary, sage, or mint, crushed; dash salt; and dash pepper.

Nutrition Facts per serving: 203 cal., 11 g total fat (2 g sat. fat), 20 mg chol., 617 mg sodium, 10 g carbo., 1 g fiber, 18 g pro.
Daily Values: 3% vit. A, 46% vit. C, 4% calcium, 6% iron

Seafood Skewers with Peanut Sauce

While the coconut milk-and-lime marinade is doing its work, you make a simple peanut sauce. Then, after just minutes on the grill, the skewers are ready to be dipped and devoured.

Prep: 20 minutes **Marinate:** 30 minutes **Grill:** 5 minutes **Serves:** 4 to 6

8 ounces fresh or frozen, peeled and deveined medium shrimp (13 to 15)
8 ounces fresh or frozen sea scallops

Marinade
¼ cup unsweetened coconut milk
2 tablespoons lime juice
1 tablespoon soy sauce

Sauce
⅓ cup unsweetened coconut milk
¼ cup peanut butter
2 tablespoons snipped fresh cilantro
1 tablespoon thinly sliced green onion
1 tablespoon lime juice
½ teaspoon chili paste or ⅛ teaspoon crushed red pepper

1 Thaw shrimp and scallops, if frozen. Rinse shrimp and scallops; pat dry with paper towels. Place in a medium bowl.

2 For marinade, in a small bowl combine the ¼ cup coconut milk, the 2 tablespoons lime juice, and the soy sauce. Pour over shrimp and scallops, stirring to coat. Cover and marinate at room temperature for 30 minutes, stirring once.

3 Meanwhile, for sauce, in a small bowl whisk together the ⅓ cup coconut milk, the peanut butter, cilantro, green onion, the 1 tablespoon lime juice, and the chili paste. Cover and let stand at room temperature for 30 minutes to blend flavors.

4 Drain shrimp and scallops, discarding marinade. On 4 to 6 metal skewers alternately thread shrimp and scallops, leaving ¼-inch spaces between pieces.

5 Lightly grease the rack of a gas grill. Preheat grill. Reduce heat to medium. Place kabobs on the grill rack directly over heat. Cover and grill for 5 to 8 minutes or until seafood is opaque, turning once halfway through grilling. Serve seafood with sauce.

Nutrition Facts per serving: 270 cal., 16 g total fat (6 g sat. fat), 104 mg chol., 542 mg sodium, 7 g carbo., 1 g fiber, 26 g pro.
Daily Values: 7% vit. A, 9% vit. C, 5% calcium, 11% iron

down by the sea

Scallops come from two places, and their size is how you can tell them apart. Sea scallops are the largest variety and are the easiest to grill. Bay scallops are smaller. No matter what kind you buy, they should be firm, sweet-smelling, and free of excess cloudy liquid. For the best flavor, refrigerate shucked scallops covered with their own liquid in a tightly sealed container for no more than 2 days.

Lobster Tails with Chive Butter

Is there anything lovelier than a lobster tail cradled in its coral-colored shell and served with melted butter? Here's proof-positive that the best things in life really are the simplest.

Prep: 10 minutes **Grill:** 12 minutes **Serves:** 4

4 **5-ounce fresh or frozen rock lobster tails**

Sauce

⅓ **cup butter**

2 **tablespoons snipped fresh chives**

1 **teaspoon finely shredded lemon peel**

Lemon wedges (optional)

1 Thaw lobster, if frozen. Rinse lobster; pat dry with paper towels. Butterfly tails by using kitchen shears or a sharp knife to cut lengthwise through centers of hard top shells and meat, cutting to, but not through, bottoms of shells. Press shell halves of tails apart with your fingers.

2 For sauce, in a small saucepan melt butter. Remove from heat. Stir in chives and lemon peel. Remove 2 tablespoons of the sauce; set the remaining sauce aside.

3 Lightly grease the rack of a gas grill. Preheat grill. Reduce heat to medium. Brush lobster meat with some of the 2 tablespoons sauce. Place lobster, meat sides down, on the grill rack directly over heat. Cover and grill for 6 minutes. Turn lobster. Brush with the rest of the 2 tablespoons sauce. Cover and grill for 6 to 8 minutes more or until lobster meat is opaque.

4 Heat the reserved sauce, stirring occasionally. Transfer the sauce to small bowls for dipping and serve with lobster. If desired, serve with lemon wedges.

Nutrition Facts per serving: 214 cal., 17 g total fat (10 g sat. fat), 118 mg chol., 395 mg sodium, 1 g carbo., 0 g fiber, 15 g pro.
Daily Values: 17% vit. A, 3% vit. C, 4% calcium, 1% iron

clarified butter is best

Though it's a nicety, not a necessity, when you have something as elegant as grilled lobster tail, clarified butter is really the classic sauce to serve.

Clarified butter, also called drawn butter, is butter with the milk solids removed. To clarify butter, melt it over low heat in a heavy saucepan without stirring. When it's completely melted, you'll see a clear, oily layer on top of a milky layer. Slowly pour the clear liquid into a dish, leaving the milky layer in the pan. The clear liquid is the clarified butter.

Grilled Mussels with Garlic Butter

Serve this San Francisco-style dish as a main course, or—divided into smaller portions—as an elegant and impressive starter for an alfresco dinner.

Prep: 50 minutes **Grill:** 5 minutes **Serves:** 4

1½ pounds fresh mussels
       (about 20)
Sauce
  ⅓ cup butter
  2 tablespoons snipped fresh
       parsley
  1 clove garlic, minced

  4 slices sourdough bread
  2 tablespoons dry white
       wine

1 Scrub mussels in shells under cold running water. If present, remove beards. In an 8-quart Dutch oven combine 4 quarts cold water and ⅓ cup salt; add mussels. Soak for 15 minutes; drain and rinse. Discard water. Repeat soaking, draining, and rinsing twice.

2 For sauce, in a small saucepan melt butter. Remove from heat. Stir in parsley and garlic. Brush both sides of bread slices with some of the sauce. Stir the wine into the remaining sauce; keep warm.

3 Preheat gas grill. Reduce heat to medium. Place bread slices on the grill rack directly over heat. Cover and grill about 2 minutes or until bread slices are toasted, turning once halfway through grilling. Remove bread from grill.

4 Place the mussels on a grill tray; add to grill. Cover and grill for 3 to 5 minutes or until shells open. Discard any that do not open. Transfer the sauce to small bowls for dipping and serve with mussels and bread.

Nutrition Facts per serving: 456 cal., 20 g total fat (11 g sat. fat), 91 mg chol., 988 mg sodium, 40 g carbo., 0 g fiber, 27 g pro.
Daily Values: 19% vit. A, 23% vit. C, 5% calcium, 43% iron

mussel magic

Mussels are sold live in the shell or fresh shucked. When buying live mussels, look for tightly closed shells that are moist, intact, and not chipped. If any of the shells are open, tap them lightly. If the mussels are alive, the shells should close. Mussels should smell fresh like the sea.

Store live mussels in the refrigerator, covered with a moist cloth, for up to 3 days. Before you cook them, discard any that aren't alive; then soak the rest in salt water and clean with a stiff brush under cold water. Right before cooking, pull off the beard between the two shells.

Burgers & Sandwiches

Gorgonzola-and-Garlic-Stuffed Burger

In This Chapter:

Gorgonzola-and-Garlic-
    Stuffed Burger 54
Grilled Pizza 64
Grilled Tuna Panini 63
Gyro Burgers 57

Herbed Focaccia with
    Chicken 60
Herbed Focaccia with
    Eggplant 60
Peanut-Sauced Chicken
    Sandwiches 61

Pork Tenderloin Wrap 59
Southwest Burger with Chile
    Salsa 55
Steak Sandwiches 56
Turkey and Grilled Corn
    Wraps 62

Gorgonzola-and-Garlic-Stuffed Burger

The burger goes uptown! Tangy blue cheese makes a creamy, melty center in these far-from-middling hamburgers. Serve 'em with gourmet potato chips and crisp raw vegetables.

Prep: 20 minutes **Grill:** 14 minutes **Serves:** 4

Burgers

½ cup crumbled Gorgonzola cheese or other blue cheese
¼ cup snipped fresh basil
1 clove garlic, minced
1¼ pounds lean ground beef
Salt and pepper

4 kaiser rolls, split and toasted
1½ cups arugula or spinach leaves
1 large tomato, sliced

1 For burgers, in a small bowl combine Gorgonzola cheese, basil, and garlic; press into 4 slightly flattened mounds. Shape ground beef into eight ¼-inch-thick patties. Place a cheese mound in centers of 4 of the patties. Top with the remaining patties; press edges to seal. Sprinkle with salt and pepper.

2 Preheat gas grill. Reduce heat to medium. Place patties on the grill rack directly over heat. Cover and grill for 14 to 18 minutes or until done (160°), turning once halfway through grilling. Serve burgers on kaiser rolls with arugula and tomato.

Nutrition Facts per serving: 467 cal., 21 g total fat (9 g sat. fat), 102 mg chol., 675 mg sodium, 33 g carbo., 2 g fiber, 35 g pro.
Daily Values: 13% vit. A, 15% vit. C, 17% calcium, 27% iron

be a burger-meister

Mastering the American art of making great grilled burgers starts with cooking them safely.

The internal color of the burger is not a reliable way to tell if it is done enough—but temperature is. A beef or pork burger needs to be cooked to 160°. Ground turkey or chicken burgers must be cooked to 165°.

An instant-read thermometer is the best tool to use to take your burger's temperature:

● If you use a digital instant-read thermometer, insert the tip of the thermometer into the food at least ⅛ of an inch for 10 seconds.

● If you use a dial instant-read thermometer, insert the thermometer through the side of the burger to a depth of 2 to 3 inches to get an accurate reading.

Southwest Burger with Chile Salsa

Can't decide whether you're in the mood for Mexican or American, tacos or burgers? Here's a little bit of both. An herbed beef burger is topped off with Monterey Jack and homemade salsa.

Prep: 30 minutes **Grill:** 14 minutes **Serves:** 4

Salsa
- 2 medium tomatoes, seeded and chopped
- ½ of a 4-ounce can diced green chile peppers, drained
- ¼ cup finely chopped onion
- ¼ cup snipped fresh cilantro
- ¼ teaspoon salt

Burgers
- 1 slightly beaten egg
- ¼ cup fine dry bread crumbs
- 2 tablespoons water
- 1 tablespoon snipped fresh oregano or 1 teaspoon dried oregano, crushed
- 1 teaspoon snipped fresh thyme or ¼ teaspoon dried thyme, crushed
- ½ teaspoon salt
- ½ teaspoon ground cumin
- ½ teaspoon chili powder
- 1 pound lean ground beef

- 4 slices Monterey Jack cheese or Monterey Jack cheese with jalapeño peppers
- 4 kaiser rolls or hamburger buns, split and toasted

1 For salsa, in a medium bowl combine tomatoes, chile peppers, onion, cilantro, and the ¼ teaspoon salt. Set aside.

2 For burgers, in a medium bowl combine egg, bread crumbs, water, oregano, thyme, the ½ teaspoon salt, the cumin, and chili powder. Add ground beef; mix well. Shape into four ¾-inch-thick patties.

3 Preheat gas grill. Reduce heat to medium. Place patties on the grill rack directly over heat. Cover and grill for 14 to 18 minutes or until done (160°), turning once halfway through grilling and adding cheese the last 1 minute of grilling. Serve burgers on kaiser rolls with salsa.

Nutrition Facts per serving: 489 cal., 22 g total fat (9 g sat. fat), 143 mg chol., 1,097 mg sodium, 38 g carbo., 3 g fiber, 34 g pro.
Daily Values: 22% vit. A, 32% vit. C, 27% calcium, 28% iron

Steak Sandwiches

The sauce on this sandwich is a French specialty. It adds a touch of sophistication and lots of flavor to this hearty, hand-held, one-dish meal.

Prep: 15 minutes **Grill:** 14 minutes **Serves:** 4

Sauce

- ¼ cup light mayonnaise dressing or salad dressing
- 1½ teaspoons finely minced gherkins
- 1 teaspoon capers, chopped
- ¼ teaspoon lemon juice
  Dash freshly ground black pepper

- 2 boneless beef top loin steaks, cut 1 inch thick (about 1 pound)
- 2 teaspoons prepared garlic spread or 2 teaspoons bottled minced garlic
- 1 large yellow sweet pepper, cut lengthwise into 8 strips
- 4 kaiser or French-style rolls, split and toasted
- 1 cup arugula or spinach leaves

1 For sauce, in a small bowl combine mayonnaise dressing, gherkins, capers, lemon juice, and the dash black pepper. Cover and refrigerate until ready to serve.

2 Trim fat from steaks. Pat steaks dry with paper towels. Rub garlic spread over both sides of steaks. Sprinkle with additional freshly ground black pepper.

3 Preheat gas grill. Reduce heat to medium. Place steaks and sweet pepper strips on the grill rack directly over heat. Cover and grill for 14 to 18 minutes or until steaks are medium rare and sweet peppers are crisp-tender, turning once halfway through grilling. Remove steaks and sweet pepper strips from grill. Cut steaks diagonally into ¼-inch slices.

4 To serve, spread the sauce on bottom halves of rolls. Top with arugula, steak slices, sweet pepper strips, and roll tops.

Nutrition Facts per serving: 380 cal., 13 g total fat (3 g sat. fat), 65 mg chol., 516 mg sodium, 37 g carbo., 0 g fiber, 29 g pro.
Daily Values: 2% vit. A, 144% vit. C, 6% calcium, 29% iron

Gyro Burgers

These burgers have all the great smoky taste of a gyro: spiced lamb, yogurt, mint, crisp cucumbers, and juicy tomatoes in an easy-to-eat, no-mess burger. A perfect prelude? Hummus and crackers.

Prep: 15 minutes **Grill:** 14 minutes **Serves:** 4

Burgers

 1 slightly beaten egg
¼ cup fine dry bread crumbs
 2 tablespoons plain yogurt
¼ teaspoon garlic salt
¼ teaspoon ground cumin
⅛ teaspoon pepper
 1 pound lean ground lamb
     or ground beef

¼ cup plain yogurt
 1 teaspoon snipped fresh
     mint
 2 large pita bread rounds,
     halved crosswise
12 thin cucumber slices
 1 medium tomato, chopped

1 For burgers, in a medium bowl combine egg, bread crumbs, the 2 tablespoons yogurt, the garlic salt, cumin, and pepper. Add ground lamb or beef; mix well. Shape into four ¾-inch-thick patties.

2 Preheat gas grill. Reduce heat to medium. Place patties on the grill rack directly over heat. Cover and grill for 14 to 18 minutes or until done (160°), turning once halfway through grilling.

3 Meanwhile, in a small bowl stir together the ¼ cup yogurt and the mint. Serve burgers in pita halves with the yogurt mixture, cucumber slices, and chopped tomato.

Nutrition Facts per serving: 373 cal., 18 g total fat (7 g sat. fat), 130 mg chol., 372 mg sodium, 25 g carbo., 1 g fiber, 26 g pro.
Daily Values: 6% vit. A, 11% vit. C, 11% calcium, 17% iron

choosing choice lamb

Lamb is a special treat at my house, and I always try to get the freshest meat I can. Whether it's ground or in any other form, it always comes from an animal less than 1 year old. You can generally gauge the tenderness and moistness of the meat by its color. The older the animal, the darker the flesh; the older the animal, the tougher the meat. For the best-tasting lamb, look for meat that is bright or light pink in color.

Tami Leonard

Test Kitchen Home Economist

Pork Tenderloin Wrap ♥

Wraps are all the rage and Asian flavors are, too. Here, flavorful pork tenderloin is rolled up with crunchy sesame-flavored slaw. Wrap up dinner with iced green tea garnished with orange slices.

Prep: 15 minutes **Marinate:** 6 hours **Grill:** 30 minutes **Stand:** 5 minutes **Serves:** 6

2 12-ounce pork tenderloins

Marinade

3 tablespoons soy sauce

2 tablespoons orange juice

1 tablespoon honey

½ teaspoon bottled minced garlic

Slaw

3 cups packaged shredded cabbage with carrot (coleslaw mix)

¼ cup thinly sliced green onions

2 tablespoons sesame seeds, toasted

1 tablespoon seasoned rice vinegar

1 teaspoon toasted sesame oil

6 12-inch plain or spinach flour tortillas*

1 Trim fat from meat. Place meat in a plastic bag set in a shallow dish. For marinade, in a small bowl combine soy sauce, orange juice, honey, and garlic. Pour over meat; seal bag. Marinate in the refrigerator for 6 hours or overnight, turning bag occasionally.

2 For slaw, in a medium bowl combine cabbage, green onions, sesame seeds, rice vinegar, and sesame oil; toss well. Cover and refrigerate until ready to serve.

3 Preheat gas grill. Adjust for indirect cooking over medium heat (see page 5). Drain tenderloin; discard marinade. Place meat on the grill rack over unlit burner. Cover and grill for 30 to 35 minutes or until meat is slightly pink in center and juices run clear. Remove meat from grill. Cover with foil; let stand for 5 minutes.

4 Thinly slice tenderloin. Arrange meat slices in a strip down the center of each tortilla. Top with slaw. Fold up bottom edge over filling; fold in sides, overlapping in the center. Serve immediately.

Nutrition Facts per serving: 319 cal., 8 g total fat (2 g sat. fat), 66 mg chol., 468 mg sodium, 28 g carbo., 2 g fiber, 32 g pro.
Daily Values: 5% vit. A, 35% vit. C, 11% calcium, 18% iron

*Note: For easier handling, wrap tortillas in heavy foil and heat on the grill about 10 minutes or until warm, turning once halfway through grilling.

Herbed Focaccia with Chicken

Bread on the grill? You bet! Italian bakers have wood-fired ovens that give their breads a woodsy flavor and an incomparably crisp crust. Use your backyard grill to get the same effect.

Prep: 20 minutes   **Rise:** 20 minutes   **Grill:** 32 minutes   **Serves:** 6

Focaccia

 - 1 16-ounce package hot roll mix
 - 4 tablespoons olive oil
 - 1 tablespoon snipped fresh basil
 - 1 teaspoon snipped fresh rosemary
 - ¼ teaspoon freshly ground black pepper

 - 1 pound skinless, boneless chicken breast halves
 - ¼ cup bottled Italian salad dressing
 - 2 or 3 plum tomatoes, cut into ¼-inch slices
 - ¼ cup shredded Parmesan cheese

1 For focaccia, prepare hot roll mix according to package directions, except substitute 2 tablespoons of the olive oil for the margarine.

2 Lightly oil a 12-inch pizza pan with 1 teaspoon of the olive oil. Press kneaded dough into pan and flatten top. Using your fingertips, press indents into top of dough. Drizzle with the remaining olive oil and sprinkle with basil, rosemary, and pepper. Cover and let rise in a warm place for 20 minutes.

3 Meanwhile, brush chicken with Italian dressing. Preheat gas grill. Reduce heat to medium. Place chicken on the grill rack directly over heat. Cover and grill for 12 to 15 minutes or until chicken is tender and no longer pink, turning once halfway through grilling. Remove from heat; cool slightly.

4 Adjust for indirect cooking over medium heat (see page 5). Place pizza pan with focaccia on the grill rack over unlit burner. Cover and grill about 15 minutes or until focaccia is puffed and beginning to brown on edges. Meanwhile, thinly slice chicken. Arrange tomato slices on top of focaccia. Top with chicken and sprinkle with Parmesan cheese. Cover and grill for 5 to 10 minutes more or until focaccia is lightly browned on edges and cheese is golden brown. Cut into wedges.

Nutrition Facts per serving: 575 cal., 24 g total fat (4 g sat. fat), 90 mg chol., 744 mg sodium, 59 g carbo., 0 g fiber, 31 g pro.
Daily Values: 5% vit. A, 7% vit. C, 6% calcium, 16% iron

Herbed Focaccia with Eggplant: Prepare as above, except substitute 1 medium eggplant for chicken. Cut eggplant into ½-inch slices; lightly coat with olive oil. Cover and grill directly over medium heat about 6 minutes or just until tender, turning once. Arrange on partially grilled focaccia with tomatoes. Top with ½ cup shredded fontina cheese in place of Parmesan cheese.

Nutrition Facts per serving: 478 cal., 19 g total fat (4 g sat. fat), 46 mg chol., 607 mg sodium, 64 g carbo., 2 g fiber, 15 g pro.
Daily Values: 6% vit. A, 8% vit. C, 6% calcium, 14% iron

Peanut-Sauced Chicken Sandwiches

Is there anyone who doesn't like peanut butter? This does the peanut butter sandwich more than one better, with spicy grilled chicken, broccoli slaw, and a peanut sauce spiked with great Asian flavor.

Prep: 15 minutes **Grill:** 12 minutes **Serves:** 4

Sauce

- 2 tablespoons sugar
- 2 tablespoons peanut butter
- 2 tablespoons soy sauce
- 2 tablespoons water
- 1 tablespoon cooking oil
- 1 clove garlic, minced

- 2 teaspoons toasted sesame oil
- ½ teaspoon crushed red pepper
- 4 medium skinless, boneless chicken breast halves (about 1 pound total)
- ½ cup packaged shredded broccoli (broccoli slaw mix)
- 4 French-style rolls, split and toasted
- ¼ cup radish sprouts (optional)
- ¼ cup chopped peanuts (optional)

1 For sauce, in a small saucepan stir together sugar, peanut butter, soy sauce, water, oil, and garlic. Cook and stir over medium heat until sugar is dissolved. Remove from heat; keep warm.

2 Combine sesame oil and crushed red pepper; brush over chicken.

3 Preheat gas grill. Reduce heat to medium. Place chicken on the grill rack directly over heat. Cover and grill for 12 to 15 minutes or until chicken is tender and no longer pink, turning once halfway through grilling.

4 To serve, place broccoli on bottom halves of rolls. Top with grilled chicken breasts, sauce, radish sprouts and peanuts if desired, and roll tops.

Nutrition Facts per serving: 360 cal., 14 g total fat (3 g sat. fat), 59 mg chol., 852 mg sodium, 29 g carbo., 1 g fiber, 28 g pro.
Daily Values: 3% vit. A, 14% vit. C, 4% calcium, 14% iron

Turkey and Grilled Corn Wraps

Corn on the cob is a classic summertime treat. Grilling gives corn on the cob a smoky flavor and caramelizes its sugars, making it sweeter than ever.

Prep: 15 minutes **Grill:** 1 hour **Stand:** 10 minutes **Serves:** 6

Sauce
- ⅔ cup bottled honey-Dijon barbecue sauce
- 1 or 2 fresh jalapeño peppers, seeded and finely chopped

- 1 1½- to 2-pound boneless turkey breast half
- 3 ears of yellow or white corn
- 2 cups shredded fresh spinach leaves
- 1 medium tomato, seeded and chopped
- ½ cup shredded carrot
- 1 tablespoon olive oil
- 1 tablespoon lime juice
- 6 10-inch flour tortillas*

1 For sauce, combine barbecue sauce and jalapeño peppers. Remove ⅓ cup of the sauce for basting. Set aside the remaining sauce until ready to serve.

2 Preheat gas grill. Adjust for indirect cooking over medium heat (see page 5). Place turkey breast on the grill rack over unlit burner. Cover and grill for 30 minutes.

3 Meanwhile, peel back the corn husks, but do not remove. Remove the corn silks; discard. Gently rinse the ears of corn. Pull the husks back up around the corn. Using 100-percent-cotton string, tie the husks shut. (If corn is purchased without husks, wrap corn in foil.) Brush some of the ⅓ cup sauce evenly over top of turkey breast. Add corn to grill around turkey. Cover and grill about 30 minutes more or until a thermometer inserted into turkey reads 170°, brushing with the rest of the ⅓ cup sauce and turning corn occasionally.

4 Remove from grill. Cover turkey with foil; let stand for 10 minutes. Meanwhile, in a medium bowl combine spinach, tomato, carrot, olive oil, and lime juice. Remove husks from corn. Cut corn kernels from cobs and add to spinach mixture; toss well.

5 Thinly slice turkey. Arrange turkey and spinach mixture near one edge of each tortilla. Drizzle with the reserved sauce. Fold up bottom edge over filling; fold in sides and roll up. Serve immediately.

Nutrition Facts per serving: 357 cal., 7 g total fat (1 g sat. fat), 74 mg chol., 702 mg sodium, 41 g carbo., 4 g fiber, 32 g pro.
Daily Values: 68% vit. A, 21% vit. C, 7% calcium, 25% iron

*Note: For easier handling, wrap tortillas in heavy foil and heat on the grill about 10 minutes or until warm, turning once halfway through grilling.

Grilled Tuna Panini

"Panini" is Italian for **"little breads"** or **"rolls."** At the train-station cafés and lunch carts of Italy, panini are often filled with cured meats and cheeses. These are fresh, light, and hot off the grill.

Prep: 15 minutes **Grill:** 6 minutes **Serves:** 4

4 4- to 6-ounce fresh tuna steaks, cut ¾ to 1 inch thick

2 tablespoons garlic-flavored oil or roasted garlic-flavored oil

Salt and pepper

1 12-inch Italian flatbread (focaccia), quartered, split horizontally, and toasted

1 recipe Giardiniera Sauce

1½ cups torn mesclun or mixed baby greens

1 medium tomato, sliced

1 Rinse fish; pat dry with paper towels. Brush both sides of fish with oil. Sprinkle with salt and pepper.

2 Lightly grease the rack of a gas grill. Preheat grill. Reduce heat to medium. Place fish on the grill rack directly over heat. Cover and grill until fish just flakes easily when tested with a fork, gently turning once halfway through grilling. (Allow 4 to 6 minutes per ½-inch thickness of fish.)

3 Place a fish steak on the grilled side of each of 4 bread pieces. Top each steak with a generous 2 tablespoons of Giardiniera Sauce, one-fourth of the greens, and a tomato slice. Top with the remaining bread pieces, grilled sides down. Serve immediately. Pass the remaining Giardiniera Sauce.

Giardiniera Sauce: In a small bowl combine ⅓ cup fat-free mayonnaise dressing or salad dressing; ⅓ cup giardiniera, drained; 3 tablespoons chopped pitted green olives; 3 cloves garlic, minced; ½ teaspoon finely shredded lemon peel; and ¼ teaspoon pepper.

Nutrition Facts per serving: 510 cal., 13 g total fat (3 g sat. fat), 19 mg chol., 813 mg sodium, 56 g carbo., 5 g fiber, 42 g pro.
Daily Values: 55% vit. A, 15% vit. C, 10% calcium, 29% iron

***Note:** "Giardiniera" is derived from the Italian *giardiniere*, or "gardener." Naturally, it refers to a crisp and colorful mix of vegetables. You'll find it in the pickle section of most supermarkets.

Grilled Pizza

Your friends will think you've gone gourmet if you make either of these grilled pizzas—one with nutty Asiago and fresh basil, the other with smoked provolone and fresh rosemary.

Prep: 25 minutes **Grill:** 10 minutes **Serves:** 4

1 16-ounce loaf frozen bread dough, thawed
Cornmeal

Asiago and Tomato Pizza

2 medium tomatoes, chopped (1½ cups)
½ cup snipped fresh basil
1 tablespoon olive oil
1 clove garlic, minced
1 cup shredded Asiago cheese
1 cup shredded mozzarella cheese

1 On a lightly floured surface, roll dough into a ¼-inch-thick circle (about 12 inches in diameter). Lightly dust both sides with cornmeal. Place on a large baking sheet dusted with cornmeal. Preheat gas grill. Reduce heat to medium. Carefully slide crust onto the grill rack directly over heat. Cover and grill about 3 minutes or until top is puffed and underside is crisp. Using a large spatula, turn crust. Cover and grill for 2 minutes.

2 Meanwhile, for toppings, in a medium bowl combine tomatoes, basil, olive oil, and garlic. Spread tomato mixture evenly over crust. Top with Asiago and mozzarella cheeses.

3 Cover and grill about 5 minutes more or until mozzarella cheese is melted and crust is cooked through.

Nutrition Facts per serving: 483 cal., 24 g total fat (11 g sat. fat), 46 mg chol., 808 mg sodium, 46 g carbo., 3 g fiber, 21 g pro.
Daily Values: 14% vit. A, 19% vit. C, 45% calcium, 18% iron

Smoked Provolone Pizza: Prepare as above, except substitute 2 teaspoons snipped fresh rosemary for the basil and use 1½ cups shredded smoked provolone or Gouda cheese in place of the Asiago and mozzarella cheeses.

Nutrition Facts per serving: 468 cal., 15 g total fat (8 g sat. fat), 29 mg chol., 374 mg sodium, 54 g carbo., .9 g fiber, 20 g pro.
Daily Values: 15% vit. A, 20% vit. C, 42% calcium, 5% iron

Starters, Sides, & Sweets

Vegetable Pizzas

In This Chapter:

Apples with Caramel Crème Fraîche 76

Grilled Banana Split 75

Grilled Chocolate-Raspberry Burritos 77

Grilled Portobellos and Onions 73

Grillside Potato Chips 70

Peaches with Quick Cherry Sauce 78

Peppers Stuffed with Goat Cheese 71

Rosemary New Potatoes 69

Sausage and Cheese Quesadillas 66

Vegetable Pizzas 68

Warm Mushroom and Leek Salad 72

Zucchini Crab Cakes 67

Sausage and Cheese Quesadillas

Here's quintessential party food: hearty sausage-and-cheese snacks that'll keep guests munching happily as the rest of dinner cooks. Top them with salsa and sour cream if you like.

Prep: 20 minutes **Grill:** 3 minutes **Serves:** 6

Filling

8 ounces bulk mild Italian sausage or chorizo
⅓ cup chopped onion
2 cloves garlic, minced
1 fresh jalapeño pepper, seeded and finely chopped

6 6- to 8-inch flour tortillas
1 tablespoon cooking oil
1 cup shredded Monterey Jack cheese
2 tablespoons snipped fresh cilantro or parsley

1 For filling, in a medium skillet cook sausage, onion, and garlic until sausage is brown and onion is tender. Drain off fat. Pat sausage mixture with paper towels to remove as much additional fat as possible. Stir in jalapeño pepper; set aside.

2 Brush one side of 3 tortillas with some of the cooking oil. Place tortillas, oil sides down, on a large baking sheet. Spread the filling over tortillas on baking sheet. Combine cheese and cilantro; sprinkle over filling. Top with the remaining tortillas. Brush tops of tortillas with the remaining oil.

3 Preheat gas grill. Reduce heat to medium. Place quesadillas on the grill rack directly over heat. Cover and grill for 3 to 4 minutes or until filling is heated through and tortillas are starting to brown, turning once halfway through grilling. To serve, cut quesadillas into wedges.

Nutrition Facts per serving: 324 cal., 23 g total fat (9 g sat. fat), 49 mg chol., 566 mg sodium, 17 g carbo., 1 g fiber, 12 g pro.
Daily Values: 6% vit. A, 5% vit. C, 21% calcium, 10% iron

Zucchini Crab Cakes

Fresh crabmeat gives these tasty tidbits the sweet taste of the sea. About 1¼ pounds of crab legs yields 8 ounces of meat. Be sure to remove and discard any small pieces of shell or cartilage.

Prep: 20 minutes **Grill:** 6 minutes **Serves:** 8

1 recipe Tomato and Sour
    Cream Sauce

Crab Cakes

1 cup coarsely shredded
    zucchini
¼ cup thinly sliced green
    onions
2 teaspoons cooking oil
1 slightly beaten egg
½ cup seasoned fine dry
    bread crumbs
1 tablespoon Dijon-style
    mustard
½ teaspoon snipped fresh
    lemon thyme or thyme
⅛ to ¼ teaspoon ground red
    pepper (optional)
8 ounces cooked fresh
    crabmeat, chopped
    (1½ cups)

2 large red and/or yellow
    tomatoes, cut into
    ¼-inch slices
    Red and/or yellow cherry
    tomatoes (optional)
    Fresh chives (optional)

1 Prepare Tomato and Sour Cream Sauce. Cover and refrigerate up to 2 hours. For crab cakes, in a large skillet cook and stir zucchini and green onions in hot oil about 3 minutes or just until vegetables are tender and liquid is evaporated. Cool slightly.

2 In a large bowl combine the egg, bread crumbs, mustard, lemon thyme, and, if desired, red pepper. Add the zucchini mixture and crabmeat; mix well. Using about ¼ cup of the mixture for each crab cake, shape into eight ½-inch-thick patties.

3 Lightly grease the rack of a gas grill. Preheat grill. Reduce heat to medium-high. Place crab cakes on the grill rack directly over heat. Cover and grill for 6 to 8 minutes or until golden brown, turning once halfway through grilling.

4 Serve the crab cakes with sliced tomatoes and sauce. If desired, garnish with cherry tomatoes and chives.

Tomato and Sour Cream Sauce: In a small bowl stir together ½ cup dairy sour cream, 3 tablespoons finely chopped yellow and/or red tomato, 1 to 2 tablespoons lemon or lime juice, and ⅛ teaspoon seasoned salt. Makes about ⅔ cup.

Nutrition Facts per serving: 119 cal., 6 g total fat (2 g sat. fat), 62 mg chol., 212 mg sodium, 8 g carbo., 1 g fiber, 9 g pro.
Daily Values: 9% vit. A, 20% vit. C, 5% calcium, 6% iron

crab-cracking 101

Buy Alaskan king crab if you want the most meat with the least hassle. The legs are up to 3 feet long and filled with long pieces of red-flecked white meat. To remove the meat from the cooked legs, use a nutcracker to crack each joint. The meat can then be easily pulled out.

Vegetable Pizzas

Visit your local farmer's market before you make these. Loaded with a gardenful of produce, these veggie-topped wedges are a fresh way to start a summer dinner on the patio.

Prep: 25 minutes **Grill:** 9 minutes **Serves:** 8

1 medium zucchini, halved
  lengthwise
1 small yellow summer
  squash, halved
  lengthwise
1 small red sweet pepper,
  halved lengthwise
2 tablespoons olive oil
1 teaspoon black pepper
½ teaspoon salt
1 large ripe tomato, seeded
  and chopped
¼ cup mayonnaise or salad
  dressing
2 tablespoons purchased
  pesto
1 tablespoon snipped fresh
  basil
1 tablespoon snipped fresh
  oregano
4 6- to 7-inch flour tortillas
1 cup shredded mozzarella
  or smoked provolone
  cheese

1 Brush zucchini, yellow squash, and red pepper halves with olive oil. Sprinkle with black pepper and salt. Preheat gas grill. Reduce heat to medium. Place vegetables on the grill rack directly over heat. Cover and grill for 6 to 8 minutes or until vegetables are crisp-tender, turning once halfway through grilling. Remove from grill; cool slightly.

2 Chop the grilled vegetables. In a medium bowl combine chopped vegetables, tomato, mayonnaise, pesto, basil, and oregano. Place tortillas on the grill rack directly over heat. Cover and grill for 1 to 2 minutes or until lightly toasted on one side. Turn tortillas over and spread the vegetable mixture over the toasted sides of tortillas. Sprinkle with shredded cheese.

3 Cover and grill for 2 to 3 minutes more or until tortillas are lightly toasted, vegetables are just heated, and cheese begins to melt. Carefully remove from grill. To serve, cut into quarters.

Nutrition Facts per serving: 201 cal., 15 g total fat (3 g sat. fat), 13 mg chol., 342 mg sodium, 12 g carbo., 1 g fiber, 6 g pro.
Daily Values: 20% vit. A, 41% vit. C, 12% calcium, 5% iron

Rosemary New Potatoes

Creamy on the inside, crisp on the outside, these herbed and buttered gems make a perfect side for nearly anything that fits on a grill: steak, chicken, pork chops, or smoked, grilled salmon.

Prep: 25 minutes **Grill:** 9 minutes **Serves:** 6 to 8

2 pounds tiny new potatoes, halved
2 tablespoons snipped fresh rosemary
2 tablespoons olive oil
2 cloves garlic, minced
1 teaspoon seasoned salt
½ teaspoon freshly ground black pepper
1 to 2 tablespoons butter, melted

1 In a covered large saucepan cook potatoes in boiling water for 12 minutes. Drain, rinse, and refrigerate.

2 Meanwhile, in a large bowl whisk together rosemary, olive oil, garlic, seasoned salt, and pepper. When potatoes are cool, add to rosemary mixture; toss gently to coat.

3 Place potatoes in a lightly greased grill pan or thread potatoes onto 6 to 8 long metal skewers, inserting skewers through sides of potatoes so the cut ends will lie flat on grill.

4 Preheat grill. Reduce heat to medium. Place grill pan or skewers on the grill rack directly over heat. Cover and grill for 9 to 10 minutes or until potatoes are browned, stirring potatoes in grill pan occasionally or turning skewers once halfway through grilling.

5 Remove potatoes from grill. Transfer to a serving dish and drizzle with melted butter.

Nutrition Facts per serving: 170 cal., 7 g total fat (2 g sat. fat), 5 mg chol., 279 mg sodium, 0 g carbo., 3 g fiber, 4 g pro.
Daily Values: 2% vit. A, 35% vit. C, 2% calcium, 7% iron

Grillside Potato Chips

These are so delicious you might not need to eat anything else. For the crispiest chips possible, use Idaho russets, which have a lower water content than most other potatoes.

Prep: 10 minutes **Grill:** 15 minutes **Stand:** 8 minutes **Serves:** 4

1 **pound potatoes (russet or long white), cut diagonally into $\frac{1}{16}$-inch slices**
3 **tablespoons cooking oil**
½ **teaspoon dried thyme, crushed**
½ **teaspoon coarse salt or seasoned salt**

1 Place potato slices in a Dutch oven. Add enough water to cover. Bring just to boiling. Cook for 2 to 3 minutes or until potatoes are crisp-tender; drain. Place in a single layer on paper towels. Carefully brush both sides of potato slices with cooking oil. Sprinkle with thyme and salt.

2 Preheat gas grill. Reduce heat to medium-high. Place potato slices on the grill rack directly over heat. Cover and grill for 15 to 20 minutes or until potatoes are browned, turning occasionally. Remove from grill. Let stand on a paper-towel-lined baking sheet for 8 to 10 minutes. (Chips will crisp as they stand.)

Nutrition Facts per serving: 209 cal., 10 g total fat (1 g sat. fat), 0 mg chol., 276 mg sodium, 27 g carbo., 1 g fiber, 3 g pro.
Daily Values: 0% vit. A, 28% vit. C, 1% calcium, 9% iron

Peppers Stuffed with Goat Cheese

Pretty and elegant and easy to do, these stuffed peppers are wonderful with grilled steak and a side of lemon-pepper pasta tossed with a little olive oil and Parmesan cheese.

Prep: 15 minutes **Grill:** 5 minutes **Serves:** 4

2 medium red, yellow, or green sweet peppers, halved lengthwise

Filling

1 ounce soft goat cheese (chèvre)

¼ cup shredded Monterey Jack cheese

1 tablespoon snipped fresh chives

1 tablespoon snipped fresh basil or 1 teaspoon dried basil, crushed

1 In a covered medium saucepan cook peppers in a small amount of boiling water for 2 minutes. Drain, cut sides down, on paper towels.

2 Meanwhile, for filling, in a small bowl combine the goat cheese, Monterey Jack cheese, chives, and basil. Spoon filling into pepper shells.

3 Fold a 24×18-inch piece of heavy foil in half to make an 18×12-inch rectangle. Place peppers in center of foil. Bring up 2 opposite edges of foil and seal with a double fold. Fold remaining ends to completely enclose peppers, leaving space for steam to build.

4 Preheat gas grill. Reduce heat to medium or medium-high. Place foil packet on the grill rack directly over heat. Cover and grill for 5 to 6 minutes or until peppers are crisp-tender and cheese is melted.

Nutrition Facts per serving: 60 cal., 4 g total fat (2 g sat. fat), 13 mg chol., 80 mg sodium, 3 g carbo., 0 g fiber, 3 g pro.
Daily Values: 30% vit. A, 104% vit. C, 4% calcium, 1% iron

Warm Mushroom and Leek Salad

Leeks—the beautifully spiraled and aromatic cousin of the scallion—get toasty brown and sweet on the grill. Here, ribbons of grilled leeks enliven a warm, Asian-style salad.

Prep: 25 minutes **Grill:** 5 minutes **Serves:** 6

Dressing
- 2 tablespoons rice wine vinegar
- 1 shallot, chopped
- 2 teaspoons honey
- 1 teaspoon soy sauce
- 1 clove garlic, minced
- ½ teaspoon toasted sesame oil
- ¼ teaspoon white pepper
- 3 tablespoons canola oil or salad oil

- 3 leeks
- 1½ pounds fresh shiitake mushrooms (use half button mushrooms, if desired)
  Lettuce leaves (optional)
- 1 tablespoon sesame seeds, toasted

1 For dressing, in a food processor bowl or blender container combine rice wine vinegar, shallot, honey, soy sauce, garlic, sesame oil, and white pepper. With machine running, slowly add canola oil. Set aside.

2 Trim roots and green leaves from leeks. In a small saucepan cook leeks in boiling water about 8 minutes or just until tender; drain and halve lengthwise. Insert a wooden pick through one end of each leek half to hold it together while grilling. Remove and discard stems from mushrooms. Rinse mushroom caps; pat dry with paper towels. Place in a grill basket.

3 Preheat gas grill. Reduce heat to medium. Place leeks and mushrooms on the grill rack directly over heat. Cover and grill for 5 to 8 minutes or until vegetables are tender, turning once halfway through grilling. Remove from grill; cool slightly.

4 Coarsely slice the vegetables. Toss the vegetables with dressing. If desired, serve the vegetable mixture on lettuce leaves. Sprinkle with sesame seed.

Nutrition Facts per serving: 157 cal., 8 g total fat (1 g sat. fat), 0 mg chol., 60 mg sodium, 22 g carbo., 3 g fiber, 2 g pro.
Daily Values: 1% vit. A, 4% vit. C, 3% calcium, 6% iron

Grilled Portobellos and Onions

These cheese-topped vegetable "medallions" are great with grilled lamb or veal. Buy similar-sized vegetables for aesthetics and so they all finish grilling at about the same time.

Prep: 15 minutes **Grill:** 7 minutes **Serves:** 4 to 6

4 fresh portobello mushrooms (about 1¼ pounds), stems removed

2 medium sweet onions

2 tablespoons olive oil

4 medium plum tomatoes, halved

1 teaspoon freshly ground black pepper

½ teaspoon salt

2 to 3 tablespoons bottled balsamic vinaigrette salad dressing

2 ounces Gorgonzola cheese or fresh mozzarella cheese, cut up

2 tablespoons snipped fresh oregano

1 Gently rinse portobello mushroom caps; pat dry with paper towels. Cut onions crosswise into ½-inch slices.

2 Brush both sides of the mushrooms and onions with olive oil. Sprinkle the mushrooms, onions, and tomato halves with pepper and salt.

3 Preheat grill. Reduce heat to medium. Place mushroom caps and onion slices on the grill rack directly over heat. Cover and grill for 6 to 8 minutes or until tender, turning once halfway through grilling. Remove from grill. Add tomatoes to grill. Cover and grill for 1 minute, turning once halfway through grilling.

4 Arrange vegetables on a serving platter. Drizzle with balsamic vinaigrette. Top with Gorgonzola cheese and sprinkle with fresh oregano.

Nutrition Facts per serving: 201 cal., 16 g total fat (4 g sat. fat), 11 mg chol., 589 mg sodium, 12 g carbo., 2 g fiber, 9 g pro.
Daily Values: 9% vit. A, 23% vit. C, 10% calcium, 8% iron

great grilled veggies

Vegetables are terrific on the grill. They get the same smoky flavor meats, poultry, and seafood do and are easy accompaniments. Here's how to grill them to perfection:

● If you use skewers, don't crowd the vegetables; leave ¼-inch spaces between pieces to ensure even cooking.

● Use separate skewers for large hunks of meat that require longer cooking times and for quick-cooking vegetables.

● Cut the vegetables into uniform sizes and shapes so they'll cook evenly.

● Use a grill basket to avoid dropping half of the veggies onto the lava rocks or briquettes. Or cover the grill rack with foil. Cut slits in the foil so vegetables grill, not stew.

Grilled Banana Split

The soda jerk never served up a banana split quite like this one! If you're in a health-conscious mood, substitute low- or nonfat vanilla frozen yogurt for the ice cream.

Soak: 30 minutes **Prep:** 20 minutes **Grill:** 5 minutes **Serves:** 4

3 medium bananas, cut into 1-inch chunks

1½ cups large strawberries, halved

1½ cups fresh pineapple chunks

1 pint vanilla ice cream

½ cup caramel and/or chocolate ice cream topping

Chopped nuts (optional)

Whipped cream (optional)

Maraschino cherries (optional)

1 Soak eight 6- or 8-inch bamboo skewers in warm water for 30 to 60 minutes; drain. Alternately thread bananas, strawberries, and pineapple onto skewers, leaving ¼-inch spaces between pieces.*

2 Preheat gas grill. Reduce heat to medium. Place kabobs on the grill rack directly over heat. Cover and grill about 5 minutes or until fruits are warm and bananas are lightly browned, turning occasionally. Remove from grill.

3 Place a scoop of ice cream and 2 fruit skewers in each serving dish. Drizzle with caramel and/or chocolate ice cream topping and, if desired, sprinkle with nuts. If desired, garnish with whipped cream and cherries.

Nutrition Facts per serving: 434 cal., 13 g total fat (8 g sat. fat), 45 mg chol., 153 mg sodium, 79 g carbo., 5 g fiber, 4 g pro.
Daily Values: 15% vit. A, 80% vit. C, 13% calcium, 4% iron

*Note: If you like, assemble the kabobs up to 1 hour ahead. Simply brush the pieces of banana with a little lemon or lime juice to prevent discoloring.

Apples with Caramel Crème Fraîche

When the air cools and the leaves begin to turn, there's nothing sweeter than this elegant take on the caramel apple. Try the sauce on grilled bananas, pineapple, or pound cake.

Prep: 15 minutes **Grill:** 8 minutes **Serves:** 6

4 Granny Smith apples, cored
4 cups water
3 tablespoons lemon juice

Crème Fraîche
½ cup whipping cream
½ cup dairy sour cream
⅓ cup caramel ice cream topping

3 tablespoons butter, melted

1 Cut apples crosswise into ½-inch slices. In a large bowl combine water and lemon juice. Soak apple slices in water mixture to prevent browning.

2 For crème fraîche, in a food processor bowl or blender container combine whipping cream, sour cream, and caramel ice cream topping. Cover and process or blend for 1 to 2 minutes or until slightly thickened. (Or beat with an electric mixer on high speed about 2 minutes or until slightly thickened.) Set aside.

3 Drain apple slices; pat dry with paper towels. Brush both sides of apples with melted butter. Preheat gas grill. Reduce heat to medium-high. Place apple slices on the grill rack directly over heat. Cover and grill for 2 minutes. Rotate apple slices a half-turn to create a checkerboard effect. Cover and grill for 2 minutes more. Turn apples over and repeat on other side.

4 To serve, arrange 3 or 4 apple slices on each dessert plate and top with crème fraîche.

Nutrition Facts per serving: 265 cal., 17 g total fat (11 g sat. fat), 51 mg chol., 118 mg sodium, 28 g carbo., 2 g fiber, 2 g pro.
Daily Values: 14% vit. A, 9% vit. C, 7% calcium, 1% iron

Grilled Chocolate-Raspberry Burritos

You love chocolate and you love to grill. Here's a sweet treat that brings the two together. Top it off with a scoop of vanilla or coffee ice cream, if you like.

Prep: 12 minutes **Grill:** 8 minutes **Serves:** 4

4 8- to 9-inch flour tortillas
1 cup semisweet chocolate pieces
1 cup fresh raspberries
2 tablespoons butter, melted
2 teaspoons sugar
½ teaspoon ground cinnamon

1 Stack the tortillas and wrap in a piece of foil. Preheat gas grill. Reduce heat to medium-low. Place foil packet on the grill rack directly over heat. Cover and grill about 5 minutes or until tortillas are warm and pliable, turning packet once halfway through grilling. Remove from grill. (Or wrap the tortillas in microwave-safe paper towels; microwave on 100% power [high] for 20 to 40 seconds.)

2 Sprinkle the chocolate pieces and raspberries in the centers of warm tortillas. Fold in sides and roll up. Brush the burritos with half of the melted butter. Place burritos on the grill rack directly over heat. Cover and grill about 3 minutes or until the tortillas begin to show grill marks and the chocolate is melted, turning once halfway through grilling.

3 Transfer the burritos to a serving platter. Brush with the remaining melted butter. In a small bowl combine the sugar and cinnamon; sprinkle over the burritos. Serve immediately.

Nutrition Facts per serving: 361 cal., 20 g total fat (4 g sat. fat), 15 mg chol., 179 mg sodium, 49 g carbo., 2 g fiber, 4 g pro.
Daily Values: 6% vit. A, 12% vit. C, 4% calcium, 15% iron

Peaches with Quick Cherry Sauce

Peaches or nectarines hold up beautifully to the heat of the grill. For the best flavor, be sure to ripen them for a few days in a paper bag before you make this fresh-fruit dessert.

Prep: 15 minutes **Grill:** 6 minutes **Serves:** 6

  3 medium peaches or
      nectarines, pitted and
      quartered
  1 tablespoon orange juice
Sauce
1½ cups fresh or thawed
      frozen unsweetened
      pitted dark sweet
      cherries
  ½ cup cherry jam
  2 tablespoons orange juice

  3 cups vanilla ice cream
  2 tablespoons coconut or
      almonds, toasted

1 Brush peaches with the 1 tablespoon orange juice. On 2 long metal skewers thread peaches, leaving ¼-inch spaces between pieces. For sauce, in a small saucepan combine cherries, cherry jam, and the 2 tablespoons orange juice. Bring to boiling over medium heat, stirring frequently; reduce heat. Simmer, uncovered, for 3 minutes. Remove from heat; keep warm.

2 Preheat gas grill. Reduce heat to medium. Place kabobs on the grill rack directly over heat. Cover and grill for 6 to 8 minutes or until peaches are heated through, turning once halfway through grilling.

3 To serve, spoon peaches and sauce over scoops of vanilla ice cream. Sprinkle with coconut.

Nutrition Facts per serving: 273 cal., 8 g total fat (5 g sat. fat), 29 mg chol., 56 mg sodium, 50 g carbo., 2 g fiber, 3 g pro.
Daily Values: 13% vit. A, 19% vit. C, 8% calcium, 3% iron

Mango-Mint Salsa

Sauces & More

In This Chapter:

Apricot Teriyaki Glaze 82
**Big-Batch Barbecue
   Sauce** 80
Grilled Corn Relish 81

Indian Curry Rub 84
Jamaican Jerk Rub 84
**Lemon-Rosemary
   Marinade** 83

Mango-Mint Salsa 82
**Pineapple-Ginger
   Marinade** 83

Big-Batch Barbecue Sauce

This barbecue sauce covers all the flavor bases—and a lot of grilled food. It's smoky, sweet, tangy, spicy, and spiked. It freezes wonderfully, so you can enjoy it now and later.

Prep: 15 minutes **Cook:** 30 minutes **Makes:** 8 cups (32 ¼-cup servings)

2½ cups water
3 6-ounce cans tomato paste
1 12-ounce bottle molasses (1½ cups)
1½ cups dark-colored corn syrup
¾ cup vinegar
¾ cup honey
2 tablespoons paprika
2 tablespoons Worcestershire sauce
2 tablespoons whiskey (optional)
1 tablespoon liquid smoke
1 tablespoon bottled hot pepper sauce
2 bay leaves
1 teaspoon garlic powder
1 teaspoon chili powder
1 teaspoon onion powder
¼ to 1 teaspoon ground red pepper

1 In a 4-quart Dutch oven combine all of the ingredients. Bring to boiling; reduce heat. Cook, uncovered, over medium-low heat for 30 minutes, stirring frequently. Remove bay leaves.

2 To use, brush beef, pork, lamb, or poultry with some of the sauce during the last 10 minutes of grilling. If desired, reheat and pass additional sauce. To store the remaining sauce, cover and refrigerate up to 2 weeks or freeze for longer storage.

Nutrition Facts per ¼ cup: 113 cal., 0 g total fat, 0 mg chol., 47 mg sodium, 29 g carbo., .6 g fiber, 1 g pro.
Daily Values: 7% vit. A, 6% vit. C, 3% calcium, 6% iron

quick and easy BBQ sauce

When you have a hankering for homemade barbecue and don't have time to stand over a simmering pot stirring in lots of ingredients, here's a super-simple, fat-free sauce.

In a saucepan combine 1 cup catsup, ½ cup water, ¼ cup finely chopped onion or 1 tablespoon dried minced onion, ¼ cup vinegar, 1 to 2 tablespoons sugar, 1 tablespoon Worcestershire sauce, ¼ teaspoon celery seed, ¼ teaspoon salt, and several dashes of bottled hot pepper sauce. Bring to boiling; reduce heat. Simmer, uncovered, for 10 to 15 minutes or to desired consistency. Brush on beef, pork, or poultry the last 10 to 20 minutes of grilling. If desired, pass any remaining sauce. Makes 1¾ cups sauce.

Grilled Corn Relish

Part salsa, part salad, this Southwest-style relish partners well with grilled chicken or pork. For a light meal, roll it up in a tortilla with black beans and shredded cheese, then warm it on the grill.

Prep: 15 minutes **Grill:** 25 minutes **Makes:** 2 cups (4 servings)

- 3 tablespoons lime juice
- 1 tablespoon cooking oil
- 2 cloves garlic, minced
- 2 ears of corn, husked and cleaned
- 1 teaspoon chili powder
- 1 small avocado, seeded, peeled, and cut up
- ½ cup chopped red sweet pepper
- ¼ cup snipped fresh cilantro
- ¼ teaspoon salt

1 In a medium bowl combine lime juice, oil, and garlic. Brush corn lightly with juice mixture. Sprinkle corn with chili powder. Preheat gas grill. Reduce heat to medium. Place corn on the grill rack directly over heat. Cover and grill for 25 to 30 minutes or until corn is tender, turning occasionally.

2 Meanwhile, add avocado, sweet pepper, cilantro, and salt to remaining lime juice mixture; toss well. Cut corn kernels from cobs and add to avocado mixture; toss well. Serve with grilled meat, poultry, or seafood.

Nutrition Facts per ½ cup: 159 cal., 12 g total fat (2 g sat. fat), 0 mg chol., 152 mg sodium, 15 g carbo., 3 g fiber, 3 g pro.
Daily Values: 15% vit. A, 51% vit. C, 1% calcium, 6% iron

Mango-Mint Salsa

Though this all-purpose salsa goes with just about everything, it's especially good on grilled fresh tuna steaks or mahi. Garnish the finished food with fresh mint, if desired.

Prep: 25 minutes **Chill:** 2 hours **Stand:** 30 minutes **Makes:** 1½ cups (6 servings)

1   ripe mango
½   cup chopped peeled
      jicama
¼   cup finely chopped red
      onion
¼   cup snipped fresh mint
1   canned chipotle pepper in
      adobo or tomato sauce,
      chopped
1   tablespoon honey
1   tablespoon olive oil

1 Peel, seed, and chop mango (you should have about 1 cup). In a medium bowl stir together mango, jicama, onion, mint, and chipotle pepper. Drizzle with honey and oil; stir to combine. Cover and refrigerate for 2 to 24 hours to blend flavors.

2 Before serving, let stand at room temperature for 30 minutes. Serve with grilled meat, poultry, fish, or seafood.

Nutrition Facts per ¼ cup: 64 cal., 2 g total fat (0 g sat. fat), 0 mg chol., 27 mg sodium, 11 g carbo., 1 g fiber, 0 g pro.
Daily Values: 27% vit. A, 25% vit. C, 1% calcium, 5% iron

Apricot Teriyaki Glaze

This sweet and gingery glaze confettied with bits of red and green sweet pepper goes with anything: chicken—as pictured on our cover—beef, or a grilled Christmas ham.

Prep: 10 minutes **Cook:** 10 minutes **Makes:** 1 cup (4 servings)

¼   cup finely chopped onion
1   clove garlic, minced
1   tablespoon cooking oil
⅔   cup apricot preserves
2   tablespoons soy sauce
2   teaspoons grated fresh
      ginger or ½ teaspoon
      ground ginger
⅓   cup finely chopped green
      sweet pepper
⅓   cup finely chopped red
      sweet pepper
½   teaspoon toasted sesame
      oil

1 In a small saucepan cook onion and garlic in hot cooking oil over medium heat for 3 minutes, stirring occasionally. Cut up any large pieces of apricot in preserves.

2 Stir apricot preserves, soy sauce, and ginger into onion mixture. Cook over medium heat until bubbly, stirring occasionally. Reduce heat. Cook, uncovered, about 10 minutes or until slightly thickened. Stir in green and red sweet pepper and sesame oil.

3 To use, brush beef, pork, lamb, or poultry with some of the glaze during the last 10 minutes of grilling. If desired, reheat and pass remaining glaze.

Nutrition Facts per ¼ cup: 200 cal., 4 g total fat (1 g sat. fat), 0 mg chol., 478 mg sodium, 40 g carbo., 1 g fiber, 2 g pro.
Daily Values: 15% vit. A, 58% vit. C, 2% calcium, 2% iron

Lemon-Rosemary Marinade

The light and refreshing lemony-herb flavor of this marinade makes it particularly well-suited to chicken or any kind of fish or seafood, such as shrimp or scallops.

Prep: 8 minutes **Marinate:** 2 hours **Makes:** about ¾ cup (enough for about 1½ pounds poultry, fish, or seafood)

1 teaspoon finely shredded
    lemon peel
⅓ cup lemon juice
¼ cup olive oil or cooking oil
¼ cup white wine
    Worcestershire sauce
1 tablespoon sugar
1 tablespoon snipped fresh
    rosemary or 1 teaspoon
    dried rosemary, crushed
¼ teaspoon salt
⅛ teaspoon pepper

1 In a small bowl stir together lemon peel, lemon juice, oil, white wine Worcestershire sauce, sugar, rosemary, salt, and pepper. To use, pour marinade over poultry, fish, or seafood in a plastic bag set in a shallow dish; seal bag.

2 Marinate in the refrigerator for 2 to 4 hours for poultry or 1 to 2 hours for fish or seafood, turning bag occasionally. Drain, reserving marinade. Grill poultry, fish, or seafood, brushing with marinade for up to the last 5 minutes of grilling. Discard any remaining marinade.

Nutrition Facts per 2 tablespoons: 97 cal., 9 g total fat (1 g sat. fat), 0 mg chol., 181 mg sodium, 5 g carbo., .1 g fiber, .3 g pro.
Daily Values: 12% vit. C, 1% calcium, 1% iron

Pineapple-Ginger Marinade

Five-spice powder, a blend of cinnamon, cloves, fennel seed, star anise, and Szechwan peppercorns used in Chinese cooking, lends an exotic touch to this fresh-tasting marinade.

Prep: 10 minutes **Marinate:** 2 hours **Makes:** about ¾ cup (enough for about 1½ pounds poultry, fish, or seafood)

½ cup unsweetened
    pineapple juice
2 tablespoons cooking oil
2 tablespoons finely
    chopped green sweet
    pepper
1 tablespoon finely chopped
    fresh ginger
1 teaspoon honey
¼ teaspoon five-spice
    powder

1 In a small bowl combine pineapple juice, cooking oil, green sweet pepper, ginger, honey, and five-spice powder. To use, pour marinade over poultry, fish, or seafood in a plastic bag set in a shallow dish; seal bag.

2 Marinate in the refrigerator for 2 to 4 hours for poultry or at room temperature for 30 minutes for fish or seafood, turning bag occasionally. Drain, reserving marinade. Grill poultry, fish, or seafood, brushing with marinade for up to the last 5 minutes of grilling. Discard any remaining marinade.

Nutrition Facts per 2 tablespoons: 57 cal., 5 g total fat (1 g sat. fat), 0 mg chol., 1 mg sodium, 4 g carbo., 0 g fiber, 0 g pro.
Daily Values: 8% vit. C, 1% calcium, 1% iron

Jamaican Jerk Rub

Culinarily speaking, the term "jerk" refers to a Jamaican manner of spicing and cooking meat or poultry. It can be wet or dry, sauced or rubbed, as is this slightly sweet and spicy blend.

Prep: 10 minutes **Makes:** about 8 teaspoons (enough for about 3 pounds meat or poultry)

2 teaspoons sugar
1½ teaspoons onion powder
1½ teaspoons dried thyme, crushed
1 teaspoon ground allspice
1 teaspoon black pepper
½ to 1 teaspoon ground red pepper
½ teaspoon salt
¼ teaspoon ground nutmeg
⅛ teaspoon ground cloves

1 In a small bowl stir together sugar, onion powder, thyme, allspice, black pepper, red pepper, salt, nutmeg, and cloves.

2 To use, sprinkle mixture evenly over meat or poultry; rub in with your fingers. Grill meat or poultry.

Nutrition Facts per teaspoon: 8 cal., 0 g total fat (0 g sat. fat), 0 mg chol., 134 mg sodium, 2 g carbo., 0 g fiber, 0 g pro.
Daily Values: 1% vit. C, 1% iron

Indian Curry Rub

This aromatic rub is essentially a homemade curry. Curries are blends of up to 20 spices that range from mild to hot and are used extensively in Indian cooking.

Prep: 10 minutes **Makes:** about ¼ cup (enough for 4 to 5 pounds meat or poultry)

2 teaspoons ground cinnamon
½ teaspoon sugar
½ teaspoon ground cumin
½ teaspoon ground turmeric
½ teaspoon ground coriander
¼ teaspoon salt
¼ teaspoon ground cardamom
¼ teaspoon ground cloves
¼ teaspoon ground nutmeg
¼ teaspoon ground red pepper

1 In a small bowl stir together cinnamon, sugar, cumin, turmeric, coriander, salt, cardamom, cloves, nutmeg, and red pepper.

2 To use, rub a little cooking oil evenly onto all sides of meat or poultry about 15 minutes before grilling. Sprinkle spice mixture evenly over meat or poultry; rub in with your fingers. Grill meat or poultry.

Nutrition Facts per teaspoon: 3 cal., 0 g total fat, 0 mg chol., 49 mg sodium, 1 g carbo., 0 g fiber, 0 g pro.
Daily Values: 1% vit. C, 1% calcium, 1% iron

Smoking

BBQ Baby Back Ribs

In This Chapter:

BBQ Baby Back Ribs 88
Hickory-Smoked Turkey 89
Salmon Salad with Chive
   Vinaigrette 91

Smoked Beef Fajitas 87
Smoked Duck Breast
   on Mixed Greens 90

Smoked Halibut with
   Hazelnut Sauce 92
Stay-Awake Steak 86

Stay-Awake Steak

You've heard of camp coffee—the kind cowboys enjoyed around the fire with a good, fresh steak. Somebody got the two together, and the result is this toasty-tasting piece of beef.

Prep: 10 minutes **Marinate:** 2 hours **Smoke:** 22 minutes **Serves:** 6

1 boneless beef top sirloin
  steak, cut 1 inch thick
  (about 1½ pounds)
Marinade
1 medium onion, chopped
½ cup bottled steak sauce or
  hickory-flavored
  barbecue sauce
¼ to ⅓ cup strong brewed
  espresso or coffee
2 tablespoons
  Worcestershire sauce

2 cups wood chips (hickory,
  pecan, or oak)
2 12-ounce cans beer or
  3 cups water

1 Trim fat from steak. Place steak in a plastic bag set in a shallow dish. For marinade, in a small bowl combine the onion, steak sauce, espresso, and Worcestershire sauce. Pour over steak; seal bag. Marinate in the refrigerator for at least 2 hours or up to 24 hours, turning bag occasionally. Drain steak, discarding marinade.

2 At least 1 hour before smoking, soak wood chips in the beer. Drain before using.

3 Preheat gas grill. Adjust for indirect cooking over medium heat (see page 5). Add soaked wood chips according to manufacturer's directions. Or, wrap in foil and add to grill (see tip, below). Cover and heat about 10 minutes or until chips begin to smoke.

4 Place steak on the grill rack over unlit burner. Cover and smoke until steak is desired doneness. (Allow 22 to 26 minutes for medium rare or 26 to 30 minutes for medium.) To serve, thinly slice the steak across the grain.

Nutrition Facts per serving: 251 cal., 17 g total fat (7 g sat. fat), 74 mg chol., 138 mg sodium, 2 g carbo., 0 g fiber, 22 g pro.
Daily Values: 1% vit. C, 1% calcium, 15% iron

clean burning

There are two ways to use hardwood chips. You can place them directly on the heating element of your gas grill, or you can make it a little easier to clean up, with no (or very little) leftover ash. Here's how:

Place soaked wood chips in the center of a 12×12-inch piece of heavy foil. Bring up two opposite edges of foil and seal with a double fold. Fold remaining ends to completely enclose chips. With a sharp knife, carefully make several small slits in top of foil packet. Place packet on the grill rack directly over heat or directly on lava rocks, ceramic briquettes, or flavorizer bars.

Smoked Beef Fajitas

These fajitas may not have the restaurant-style drama of a smoking, sizzling dining-room entrance, but their great smoked flavor more than makes up for it. Homemade Pico de Gallo is a fresh touch.

Prep: 15 minutes   **Marinate:** 6 hours   **Smoke:** 18 minutes   **Serves:** 4

1   1- to 1¼-pound beef flank steak

Marinade
1   cup beer
1   medium onion, chopped
½   cup lime juice
3   tablespoons cooking oil
2   tablespoons bottled steak sauce
1   tablespoon chili powder
1   teaspoon ground cumin
1   bay leaf
4   cloves garlic, minced

1   recipe Pico de Gallo
2   cups wood chips (oak or hickory)
8   7-inch flour or corn tortillas
3   red, yellow, and/or green sweet peppers, cut into thin strips

1 Trim fat from steak. Score steak by making shallow diagonal cuts at 1-inch intervals in a diamond pattern. Repeat on other side. Place steak in a plastic bag set in a shallow dish.

2 For marinade, in a medium bowl combine beer, onion, lime juice, oil, steak sauce, chili powder, cumin, bay leaf, and garlic. Pour over steak; seal bag. Marinate in the refrigerator for 6 to 24 hours, turning bag occasionally. Drain steak, discarding marinade. Prepare Pico de Gallo. Cover and refrigerate for up to 24 hours. At least 1 hour before smoking, soak wood chips in enough water to cover. Drain before using.

3 Stack tortillas and wrap in a piece of foil. Fold a 24×18-inch piece of heavy foil in half to make an 18×12-inch rectangle. Place pepper strips in center of foil. Bring up 2 opposite edges of foil and seal with a double fold. Fold remaining ends to completely enclose peppers, leaving space for steam to build.

4 Preheat gas grill. Adjust for indirect cooking over medium heat (see page 5). Add soaked wood chips according to manufacturer's directions. Or wrap in foil and add to grill (see tip, page 86). Cover and heat about 10 minutes or until chips begin to smoke. Place steak and tortilla packet on the grill rack over unlit burner. Place pepper packet on the grill rack directly over heat. Cover and smoke until steak is desired doneness. (Allow 18 to 22 minutes for medium.)

5 To serve, thinly slice steak across the grain. Divide steak and peppers among tortillas; fold up. Serve with Pico de Gallo.

Pico de Gallo: Stir together 2 plum tomatoes, chopped; ¼ of a medium cucumber, seeded and chopped; 2 green onions, sliced; 2 tablespoons snipped fresh cilantro; 1 fresh serrano pepper, seeded and chopped; and ⅛ teaspoon salt.

Nutrition Facts per serving: 450 cal., 19 g total fat (6 g sat. fat), 58 mg chol., 423 mg sodium, 41 g carbo., 4 g fiber, 28 g pro.
Daily Values: 54% vit. A, 331% vit. C, 10% calcium, 28% iron

BBQ Baby Back Ribs

Here's the quintessential barbecue experience that no barbecue king could top short of digging a pit and roasting a whole pig. And you can do it right in your own backyard.

Prep: 15 minutes   **Soak:** 1 hour   **Smoke:** 1½ hours   **Serves:** 6 to 8

    4 **cups wood chips (apple or hickory)**
    4 **pounds pork loin back ribs or meaty spareribs**
Rub
    2 **tablespoons barbecue seasoning**
    1 **tablespoon garlic powder**
    1 **teaspoon onion salt**
    ½ **teaspoon celery seed, ground**
    ¼ **teaspoon ground red pepper**

    ½ to ¾ cup bottled barbecue sauce

1 At least 1 hour before smoking, soak wood chips in enough water to cover. Drain before using.

2 Trim fat from ribs. For rub, in a small bowl stir together the barbecue seasoning, garlic powder, onion salt, celery seed, and red pepper. Sprinkle seasoning mixture evenly over ribs; rub in with your fingers.

3 Preheat gas grill. Adjust for indirect cooking over medium heat (see page 5). Add soaked wood chips according to manufacturer's directions. Or wrap in foil and add to grill (see tip, page 86). Cover and heat about 10 minutes or until chips begin to smoke.

4 Place ribs, bone sides down, in a roasting pan; set the pan on the grill rack over unlit burner. (Or place ribs in a rib rack; place on grill rack over unlit burner.) Cover and smoke for 1½ to 2 hours or until ribs are very tender. Cut ribs into serving-size pieces. Heat the barbecue sauce and pass with ribs.

Nutrition Facts per serving: 454 cal., 33 g total fat (12 g sat. fat), 77 mg chol., 678 mg sodium, 6 g carbo., .8 g fiber, 32 g pro.
Daily Values: 11% vit. A, 5% vit. C, 4% calcium, 11% iron

Hickory-Smoked Turkey

Fight over the legs of this magnificent smoked bird, then savor the leftover breast, sliced and served in a sandwich with a drift of mayonnaise and slices of fresh tomato and spicy radish sprouts.

Prep: 15 minutes **Soak:** 1 hour **Smoke:** 2¾ hours **Stand:** 15 minutes **Serves:** 12 to 14

4 cups wood chips (hickory or oak)
1 10- to 12-pound turkey
2 tablespoons olive oil
1 teaspoon dried thyme, crushed
1 teaspoon dried sage, crushed
½ teaspoon salt
¼ teaspoon pepper

1 At least 1 hour before smoking, soak wood chips in enough water to cover. Drain before using.

2 Remove neck and giblets from turkey. Rub skin of turkey with oil. Sprinkle inside and out with thyme, sage, salt, and pepper. Skewer the neck skin to the back. Twist wing tips under back. Tuck drumsticks under the band of skin across the tail, or tie the legs to tail with 100-percent-cotton string. Insert a meat thermometer into the center of an inside thigh muscle without allowing it to touch bone.

3 Preheat gas grill. Adjust for indirect cooking over medium heat (see page 5). Add soaked wood chips according to manufacturer's directions. Or wrap in foil and add to grill (see tip, page 86). Cover and heat about 10 minutes or until chips begin to smoke.

4 Place turkey, breast side up, on a rack in a roasting pan; set the pan on the grill rack over unlit burner. Cover and smoke for 2¾ to 3½ hours or until the meat thermometer registers 180°. Cut band of skin or string between drumsticks after 1¾ hours of cooking. Remove turkey from grill. Cover with foil; let stand for 15 minutes before carving.

Nutrition Facts per serving: 277 cal., 14 g total fat (4 g sat. fat), 120 mg chol., 173 mg sodium, 0 g carbo., 0 g fiber, 35 g pro.
Daily Values: 8% vit. A, 2% calcium, 17% iron

Smoked Duck Breast on Mixed Greens

Duck—with its moist and flavorful flesh—takes particularly well to smoking. Here it highlights a Chinese-inspired salad of greens, mandarin oranges, mushrooms, and toasted almonds.

Prep: 25 minutes   **Soak:** 1 hour   **Smoke:** 15 minutes   **Serves:** 4

2   cups wood chips (oak, apple, or pecan)

Dressing
⅓   cup rice wine vinegar or white wine vinegar
4   teaspoons soy sauce
2   cloves garlic, minced
½   teaspoon toasted sesame oil
¼   cup cooking oil

4   5- to 6-ounce skinless, boneless duck breast halves
    Salt and pepper
9   cups torn mixed salad greens
1   cup fresh shiitake mushrooms, stemmed and sliced
1   11-ounce can mandarin orange sections, drained
½   cup sliced almonds, toasted

1 At least 1 hour before smoking, soak wood chips in enough water to cover. Drain before using.

2 For dressing, in a food processor bowl or blender container combine rice wine vinegar, soy sauce, garlic, and sesame oil. With the machine running, slowly add cooking oil. Set aside.

3 Preheat gas grill. Adjust for indirect cooking over medium heat (see page 5). Add soaked wood chips according to manufacturer's directions. Or wrap in foil and add to grill (see tip, page 86). Cover and heat about 10 minutes or until chips begin to smoke.

4 Sprinkle duck with salt and pepper. Place duck on the grill rack over unlit burner. Cover and smoke for 15 to 18 minutes or until duck is no longer pink and juices run clear.

5 In a large bowl combine salad greens, mushrooms, oranges, and almonds. Stir dressing. Pour half of the dressing over greens mixture; toss gently to coat. Divide mixture among 4 dinner plates. Slice smoked duck and arrange on top of greens mixture. Pass the remaining dressing.

Nutrition Facts per serving: 437 cal., 26 g total fat (3 g sat. fat), 122 mg chol., 487 mg sodium, 22 g carbo., 6 g fiber, 31 g pro.
Daily Values: 31% vit. A, 88% vit. C, 15% calcium, 38% iron

Salmon Salad with Chive Vinaigrette

Smoked salmon is the height of elegance. Paired with a shallot-and-chive vinaigrette and fancy baby greens, it's great company fare. Serve it with sourdough bread and chilled white wine.

Prep: 20 minutes **Soak:** 1 hour **Smoke:** 22 minutes **Serves:** 4

2 cups wood chips (alder or hickory)

Vinaigrette

2 shallots, chopped
¼ cup rice vinegar
2 tablespoons lime juice
4 teaspoons sugar
½ teaspoon salt
½ cup olive oil
2 tablespoons snipped fresh chives

1 1½-pound fresh or frozen skinless, boneless salmon fillet, ¾ to 1 inch thick
1 tablespoon snipped fresh dill
½ teaspoon salt
½ teaspoon pepper
8 ounces mesclun or torn mixed salad greens

1 At least 1 hour before smoking, soak wood chips in enough water to cover. Drain before using.

2 For vinaigrette, in a food processor bowl or blender container combine shallots, rice vinegar, lime juice, sugar, and ½ teaspoon salt. With machine running, slowly add oil. Add chives; process or blend with one or two on-off pulses just to mix. Set aside.

3 Thaw fish, if frozen. Rinse fish; pat dry with paper towels. Sprinkle fish with dill, ½ teaspoon salt, and the pepper. Cut several slits in a piece of heavy foil large enough to hold fish. Grease foil; place fish on foil, tucking under any thin edges.

4 Preheat gas grill. Adjust for indirect cooking over medium heat (see page 5). Add soaked wood chips according to manufacturer's directions. Or wrap in foil and add to grill (see tip, page 86). Cover and heat about 10 minutes or until chips begin to smoke. Place foil with fish on grill rack over unlit burner. Cover and smoke until fish just flakes easily when tested with a fork. (Allow 15 to 18 minutes per ½-inch thickness of fish.)

5 Stir vinaigrette. In a large bowl pour half of the vinaigrette over mesclun; toss to coat. Divide mesclun among 4 dinner plates. Cut fish into 4 serving-size pieces and arrange on top of mesclun. If desired, pass the remaining vinaigrette. To store any leftover vinaigrette, cover and refrigerate for up to 1 week.

Nutrition Facts per serving: 390 cal., 24 g total fat (4 g sat. fat), 76 mg chol., 666 mg sodium, 5 g carbo., 1 g fiber, 38 g pro.
Daily Values: 9% vit. A, 9% vit. C, 8% calcium, 8% iron

Smoked Halibut with Hazelnut Sauce

Nut butters (not the peanut butter variety, but toasted nuts in melted butter) are wonderful, simple accompaniments to grilled fish, smoked or not. Try this recipe with pistachios.

Prep: 20 minutes **Soak:** 1 hour **Smoke:** 30 minutes **Serves:** 4

2 cups wood chips (apple, pecan, or oak)

3 cups apple juice or water

4 6-ounce fresh or frozen halibut steaks, cut 1 inch thick

Sauce

⅓ cup butter

⅓ cup chopped blanched hazelnuts (filberts)

1 tablespoon apple juice or dry white wine

1 tablespoon snipped fresh parsley (optional)

1 At least 1 hour before smoking, soak wood chips in the 3 cups apple juice. Drain before using.

2 Thaw fish, if frozen. Rinse fish; pat dry with paper towels. Lightly grease the rack of a gas grill. Preheat grill. Adjust for indirect cooking over medium heat (see page 5). Add soaked wood chips according to manufacturer's directions. Or, wrap in foil and add to grill (see tip, page 86). Cover and heat about 10 minutes or until chips begin to smoke.

3 Place fish on the grill rack over unlit burner. Cover and smoke until fish flakes easily when tested with a fork. (Allow 15 to 18 minutes per ½-inch thickness of fish.) Remove from grill; keep warm.

4 For sauce, in a small skillet melt butter over medium heat. Add hazelnuts and cook, stirring occasionally, until nuts are toasted and butter is browned but not burned. Remove from heat. Stir in the 1 tablespoon apple juice. Serve immediately over grilled fish. If desired, garnish with parsley.

Nutrition Facts per serving: 402 cal., 27 g total fat (11 g sat. fat), 98 mg chol., 257 mg sodium, 2 g carbo., 1 g fiber, 37 g pro.
Daily Values: 22% vit. A, 1% vit. C, 10% calcium, 11% iron

what sort of wood?

The kind of hardwood chips you use to smoke your meat, poultry, or fish is really up to you. Some smoke flavors, however, seem to pair more naturally with some kinds of food than others. In general, mesquite is best with beef, though oak and hickory are nice. Hickory, apple wood, and pecan are perfect with pork. Hickory is a natural with chicken and turkey. And most salmon-smokers wouldn't think of using anything but alder or apple woods.

INDEX

Photographs indicated in **bold**.

A-B

Appetizers.
Grilled Mussels with Garlic
Butter, 52
Sausage and Cheese
Quesadillas, 66
Vegetable Pizzas, **65, 68**
Zucchini Crab Cakes, 67
Apple Filling, Chicken Rolls with,
27, 30 ♥
Apples with Caramel Crème
Fraîche, 76
Apricot Teriyaki Glaze, 82
Banana Split, Grilled, **74, 75**
barbecuing vs. grilling, 22
Basil.
Basil-Stuffed Beef, 16
Chicken with Garlic and
Basil, **34**
Fish with Orange-Basil
Salsa, 49
Beef. *See also* Burgers; Steaks
Basil-Stuffed Beef, 16
Beef and Blue Cheese Salad, **13**
Horseradish-Rubbed Beef
Tenderloin, 15
Smoked Beef Fajitas, **87**
Burgers.
Burger with Chile Salsa,
Southwest, 55
Gorgonzola-and-Garlic-Stuffed
Burger, **53, 54**
Gyro Burgers, 57
safety guidelines, 54
burners, igniting, 5
Burritos, Grilled Chocolate-
Raspberry, 77
Butter.
clarified, 51
Grilled Mussels with Garlic
Butter, 52
Lobster Tails with Chive
Butter, **41, 51**

C

charring, avoiding excess, 5
Cheese.
Beef and Blue Cheese Salad, **13**
Gorgonzola-and-Garlic-Stuffed
Burger, **53, 54**
Grilled Pizza, 64
Peppers Stuffed with Goat
Cheese, 71
Sausage and Cheese
Quesadillas, 66
Smoked Provolone Pizza, 64
Turkey Tenderloins, Stuffed, 38
Cherry Sauce, Peaches with
Quick, 78
Chicken.
Barbecue Chicken, Finger-
Lickin', 28
Chicken and Citrus Salad, 35 ♥
Chicken and Pasta, Provençal,
32, **33**
Chicken Rolls with Apple
Filling, **27, 30** ♥
Chicken Thighs, Greek, 31
Chicken with Garlic
and Basil, **34**
Herbed Focaccia with
Chicken, 60
Peanut-Sauced Chicken
Sandwiches, **61**
Tandoori Chicken, 29
chips, hardwood, 86, 92
Chocolate-Raspberry Burritos,
Grilled, 77
Citrus Salad, Chicken and, 35 ♥
cooking times, 6, (see inside front
and back covers)
Cornish hens.
Game Hens with Grilled
Peppers, 40
Corn Relish, Grilled, **81**
Corn Wraps, Turkey and Grilled,
62 ♥
Crab Cakes, Zucchini, 67
crab, removing meat from, 67
Crème Fraîche, Apples with
Caramel, 76

D-F

Desserts.
Apples with Caramel Crème
Fraîche, 76
Grilled Banana Split, **74,** 75
Grilled Chocolate-Raspberry
Burritos, 77
Peaches with Quick Cherry
Sauce, 78
direct grilling, 5, 22
Duck Breast on Mixed Greens,
Smoked, 90
Eggplant, Herbed Focaccia
with, 60
Fajitas, Smoked Beef, **87**
**Fish and seafood. *See also*
Salmon**
doneness, testing for, 46
Grilled Mussels with Garlic
Butter, 52
Grilled Tuna Niçoise Salad,
44, **45**
Grilled Tuna Panini, 63
Lime-Marinated Halibut, 43 ♥
Lobster Tails with Chive Butter,
41, 51
Red Snapper with Herb-Pecan
Crust, 46
Seafood Skewers with Peanut
Sauce, 50
Smoked Halibut with Hazelnut
Sauce, 92
Wasabi-Glazed Whitefish, **48** ♥
Zucchini Crab Cakes, 67
Focaccia.
Grilled Tuna Panini, 63
Herbed Focaccia with
Chicken, 60
Herbed Focaccia with
Eggplant, 60
Fruit. *See specific kinds*

G

Game Hens with Grilled
Peppers, 40
Garlic.
Chicken with Garlic and
Basil, **34**
Gorgonzola-and-Garlic-Stuffed
Burger, **53,** 54
Grilled Mussels with Garlic
Butter, 52
Rib Eyes with Grilled Garlic, 9
Giardiniera Sauce, 63
Glaze, Apricot Teriyaki, 82
Gorgonzola-and-Garlic-Stuffed
Burger, **53,** 54
grilling charts, (see inside front
and back covers)
grilling vs. barbecuing, 22
grill tips, 5–6

H-L

Halibut, Lime-Marinated, 43 ♥
Halibut with Hazelnut Sauce,
Smoked, 92
Hazelnut Sauce, Smoked Halibut
with, 92
herb blends, 32
Herb-Lemon Marinade, 49
Horseradish-Rubbed Beef
Tenderloin, 15
indirect grilling, 5, 22
Jerk Pork, 20 ♥
Jerk Rub, Jamaican, 84
Kabobs.
Pork Satay, Thai, **7, 21**
Seafood Skewers with Peanut
Sauce, 50
tips, 26, 73
Veal Brochettes,
Mediterranean, 26 ♥
Lamb.
buying, 57
Grilled Greek Leg of Lamb, 23
Gyro Burgers, 57
Lamb Chops, Mongolian-
Style, **25**

Minted Lamb Chops,
Fragrant, 24
Leek Salad, Warm Mushroom
and, **72**
Lemon Marinade, Herb-, 49
Lemon-Rosemary Marinade, 83
Lime-Marinated Halibut, 43 ♥
Lobster Tails with Chive Butter,
41, 51

M-O

Mango-Mint Salsa, **79,** 82
Marinades.
facts about, 42
Herb-Lemon Marinade, 49
Lemon-Rosemary Marinade, 83
Marinade, Southeast Asian, 49
Pineapple-Ginger Marinade, 83
Mushrooms.
Grilled Portobellos and
Onions, 73
Mushroom and Leek Salad,
Warm, **72**
mussels, buying and cooking, 52
Mussels with Garlic Butter,
Grilled, 52
Mustard Sauce, Peppercorn-, 14
Onions.
Beef and Blue Cheese Salad, **13**
Grilled Portobellos and
Onions, 73
Orange-Basil Salsa, Fish
with, 49

P-R

Pasta, Provençal Chicken and,
32, **33**
Peaches with Quick Cherry
Sauce, 78
Peanut Sauce, Seafood Skewers
with, 50
Pecan Crust, Red Snapper with
Herb-, 46
pepper, black, 14
Peppercorns.
facts about, 14
Filet Mignon with Peppercorn
Sauce, 14
Peppercorn-Mustard Sauce, 14

Peppers, Game Hens with
Grilled, 40
Peppers Stuffed with Goat
Cheese, 71
Pesto, Turkey with Cilantro, 39
Pico de Gallo, **87**
Pineapple-Ginger Marinade, 83
Pizzas.
Grilled Pizza, 64
Smoked Provolone Pizza, 64
Vegetable Pizzas, **65, 68**
Pork.
Barbecued Chops, South
Carolina, **18,** 19
BBQ Baby Back Ribs, **85, 88**
Jerk Pork, 20 ♥
Peppery Pork Chops, 17
Pork Satay, Thai, **7, 21**
Pork Tenderloin Wrap, **58,** 59 ♥
Sweet and Spicy BBQ Ribs,
22 ♥
Portobellos and Onions,
Grilled, 73
Potato Chips, Grillside, **70**
Potatoes, Rosemary New, 69
poultry, safety guidelines for, 29
preheating grill, 5
Provolone Pizza, Smoked, 64
Quesadillas, Sausage and
Cheese, 66
Raspberry Burritos, Grilled
Chocolate-, 77
Red Snapper with Herb-Pecan
Crust, 46
Relish, Grilled Corn, **81**
Ribs, BBQ Baby Back, **85, 88**
Rub, Indian Curry, 84
Rub, Jamaican Jerk, 84

S

safety guidelines, 12, 29, 54
Salads.
Beef and Blue Cheese Salad, **13**
Chicken and Citrus Salad, 35 ♥
Grilled Tuna Niçoise Salad,
44, **45**
Mushroom and Leek Salad,
Warm, 72
Salmon Salad with Chive
Vinaigrette, 91

Smoked Duck Breast on Mixed
   Greens, 90
Salmon.
   Fish and Vegetable Packets, 47
   Fish with Orange-Basil
      Salsa, 49
   Salmon Salad with Chive
      Vinaigrette, 91
   Sesame-Ginger Grilled
      Salmon, 42
Salsa.
   Burger with Chile Salsa,
      Southwest, 55
   Fish with Orange-Basil
      Salsa, 49
   Mango-Mint Salsa, **79, 82**
Sandwiches.
   Grilled Tuna Panini, 63
   Peanut-Sauced Chicken
      Sandwiches, **61**
   Pork Tenderloin Wrap, **58, 59** ♥
   Smoked Beef Fajitas, **87**
   Steak Sandwiches, 56
   Turkey and Grilled Corn
      Wraps, 62 ♥
Satay Sauce, **7, 21**
Sauces.
   Barbecue Sauce, Big-Batch, 80
   Peppercorn-Mustard Sauce, 14
   quick and easy BBQ sauce, 80
   Satay Sauce, **7, 21**
   Tomato and Sour Cream
      Sauce, 67
   Sausage and Cheese
      Quesadillas, 66
Scallops, facts about, 50
Seafood. *See* **Fish and seafood**
Sesame-Ginger Grilled
   Salmon, 42
Skewers. *See* **Kabobs**
Sour Cream Sauce, Tomato
   and, 67
Steaks.
   Filet Mignon with Peppercorn
      Sauce, 14
   Flank Steak, Mexican Fiesta, 11
   Grilled Steak with Martini
      Twist, **10** ♥
   Rib Eyes with Grilled Garlic, 9

Smoked Beef Fajitas, **87**
Steak Sandwiches, 56
Steak, Stay-Awake, 86
Steaks, Garlic-Barbecued, 12
Teriyaki T-Bone Steaks, **8, on
   back cover**

T-U

temperature, estimating, 6
Teriyaki Glaze, Apricot, 82
Teriyaki T-Bone Steaks, **8, on
   back cover**
Tomato and Sour Cream
   Sauce, 67
Tortillas.
   Flank Steak, Mexican Fiesta, 11
   Grilled Chocolate-Raspberry
      Burritos, 77
   Pork Tenderloin Wrap, **58, 59** ♥
   Sausage and Cheese
      Quesadillas, 66
   Smoked Beef Fajitas, **87**
   Turkey and Grilled Corn
      Wraps, 62 ♥
   Vegetable Pizzas, **65, 68**
Tuna Niçoise Salad, Grilled,
   44, **45**
Tuna Panini, Grilled, 63
Turkey.
   Grilled Turkey Piccata, **36,
      37** ♥
   Hickory-Smoked Turkey, 89
   tenderloin steaks, substitution
      for, 37
   Turkey and Grilled Corn
      Wraps, 62 ♥
   Turkey Tenderloins, Stuffed, 38
   Turkey with Cilantro Pesto, 39

V-Z

Veal Brochettes, Mediterranean,
   26 ♥
Vegetables. *See also specific
   kinds*
   Chicken and Pasta, Provençal,
      32, **33**
   Fish and Vegetable Packets, 47
   Grilled Corn Relish, **81**
   Grilled Tuna Niçoise Salad,
      44, **45**

grilling tips, 73
Smoked Duck Breast on Mixed
   Greens, 90
Vegetable Pizzas, **65, 68**
Wasabi-Glazed Whitefish, **48** ♥
Vinaigrette, Salmon Salad with
   Chive, 91
Wasabi-Glazed Whitefish, **48** ♥
Zucchini Crab Cakes, 67

Tips

accessories, grill, 35
barbecuing vs. grilling, 22
black pepper, facts about, 14
burgers, safety guidelines for, 54
burners, igniting, 5
butter, clarified, 51
charring, avoiding excess, 5
chips, hardwood, 86, 92
cooking times, 6
crab, removing meat from, 67
direct grilling, 5, 22
fish, testing for doneness, 46
grill, cleaning, 6
grill, covering, 5
grill, turning off, 6
grilling charts, (see inside front
and back covers)
herb blends, 32
indirect grilling, 5, 22
kabobs, 26, 73
lamb, buying, 57
marinades, facts about, 42
mussels, buying and cooking, 52
peppercorns, facts about, 14
poultry, safety guidelines for, 29
preheating grill, 5
quick and easy BBQ sauce, 80
safety guidelines, 12, 29, 54
scallops, facts about, 50
temperature, estimating, 6
turkey tenderloin, substitution
   for, 37
vegetables, grilling, 73, (see inside
back cover)

Metric Cooking Hints

By making a few conversions, cooks in Australia, Canada, and the United Kingdom can use the recipes in this book with confidence. The charts on this page provide a guide for converting measurements from the U.S. customary system, which is used throughout this book, to the imperial and metric systems. There also is a conversion table for oven temperatures to accommodate the differences in oven calibrations.

Product Differences: Most of the ingredients called for in the recipes in this book are available in English-speaking countries. However, some are known by different names. Here are some common U.S. ingredients and their possible counterparts:
● Sugar is granulated or castor sugar.
● Powdered sugar is icing sugar.
● All-purpose flour is plain household flour or white four. When self-rising flour is used in place of all-purpose flour in a recipe that calls for leavening, omit the leavening agent (baking soda or baking powder) and salt.
● Light-colored corn syrup is golden syrup.
● Cornstarch is cornflour.
● Baking soda is bicarbonate of soda.
● Vanilla is vanilla essence.
● Green, red, or yellow sweet peppers are capsicums.
● Golden raisins are sultanas.

Volume and Weight: U.S. Americans traditionally use cup measures for liquid and solid ingredients. The chart, right, shows the approximate imperial and metric equivalents. If you are accustomed to weighing solid ingredients, the following approximate equivalents will help.
● 1 cup butter, castor sugar, or rice = 8 ounces = about 230 grams
● 1 cup flour = 4 ounces = about 115 grams
● 1 cup icing sugar = 5 ounces = about 140 grams

Spoon measures are used for smaller amounts of ingredients. Although the size of the tablespoon varies slightly in different countries, for practical purposes and for recipes in this book, a straight substitution is all that's necessary.

Measurements made using cups or spoons always should be level unless stated otherwise.

Equivalents: U.S. = U.K./Australia

⅛ teaspoon = 1 ml
¼ teaspoon = 1.25 ml
½ teaspoon = 2.5 ml
1 teaspoon = 5 ml
1 tablespoon = 15 ml
1 fluid ounce = 30 ml
¼ cup = 60 ml
⅓ cup = 80 ml
½ cup = 120 ml
⅔ cup = 160 ml
¾ cup = 180 ml
1 cup = 240 ml
2 cups = 475 ml
1 quart = 1 liter
½ inch = 1.25 cm
1 inch = 2.5 cm

Baking Pan Sizes

U.S.	Metric
8×1½-inch round baking pan	20×4-cm cake tin
9×1½-inch round baking pan	23×4-cm cake tin
11×7×1½-inch baking pan	28×18×4-cm baking tin
13×9×2-inch baking pan	32×23×5-cm baking tin
2-quart rectangular baking dish	28×18×4-cm baking tin
15×10×1-inch baking pan	38×25×2.5-cm baking tin (Swiss roll tin)
9-inch pie plate	22×4- or 23×4-cm pie plate
7- or 8-inch springform pan	18- or 20-cm springform or loose-bottom cake tin
9×5×3-inch loaf pan	23×13×8-cm or 2-pound narrow loaf tin or pâté tin
1½-quart casserole	1.5-liter casserole
2-quart casserole	2-liter casserole

Oven Temperature Equivalents

Fahrenheit Setting:	Celsius Setting*:	Gas Setting:
300°F	150°C	Gas Mark 2 (very low)
325°F	170°C	Gas Mark 3 (low)
350°F	180°C	Gas Mark 4 (moderate)
375°F	190°C	Gas Mark 5 (moderately hot)
400°F	200°C	Gas Mark 6 (hot)
425°F	220°C	Gas Mark 7 (hot)
450°F	230°C	Gas Mark 8 (very hot)
475°F	240°C	Gas Mark 9 (very hot)
Broil		Grill

*Electric and gas ovens may be calibrated using Celsius. However, for an electric oven, increase the Celsius setting 10 to 20 degrees when cooking above 160°C. For convection or forced-air ovens (gas or electric), lower the temperature setting 10°C when cooking at all heat levels.

rush!
free-year request

BUSINESS REPLY MAIL
FIRST-CLASS MAIL PERMIT NO. 120 BOONE, IA

POSTAGE WILL BE PAID BY ADDRESSEE

Better Homes and Gardens®
Hometown
Cooking™

MAGAZINE
PO BOX 37456
BOONE IA 50037-2456

rush!
free-year request

BUSINESS REPLY MAIL
FIRST-CLASS MAIL PERMIT NO. 120 BOONE, IA

POSTAGE WILL BE PAID BY ADDRESSEE

Better
Homes
and Gardens ®

MAGAZINE
PO BOX 37428
BOONE IA 50037-2428